Recipes From Momma's Kitchen

By Helen Salyer Perkins

Recipes From Momma's Kitchen by Helen Salyer Perkins

Copyright © 2018. All rights reserved.

ALL RIGHTS RESERVED: No part of this book may be reproduced, stored, or transmitted, in any form, without the express and prior permission in writing of Pen It! Publications. This book may not be circulated in any form of binding or cover other than that in which it is currently published.

This book is licensed for your personal enjoyment only. All rights are reserved. Pen It! Publications does not grant you rights to resell or distribute this book without prior written consent of both Pen It! Publications and the copyright owner of this book. This book must not be copied, transferred, sold or distributed in any way.

Disclaimer: Neither Pen It! Publications, or our authors will be responsible for repercussions to anyone who utilizes the subject of this book for illegal, immoral or unethical use.

This book of recipes are from the author's collection of recipes written by herself, friends and ones that have been passed down over the years. Any likeness to other recipes is purely coincidental.

This book or part thereof may not be reproduced in any form, stored in a retrieval system, or transmitted in any form by any means-electronic, mechanical, photocopy, recording or otherwise-without prior written consent of the publisher, except as provided by United States of America copyright law.

Published by Pen It! Publications, LLC
812-371-4128   www.penitpublications.com

Published in the United States of America by Pen It! Publications, LLC

ISBN: 978-1-949609905

Dedication

I thank God for giving me the desire and ability to accumulate
so many interesting and delicious recipes to share.
To my wonderful family and friends who have so generously
shared their favorite recipes to help make this recipe collection so
very special and unique.
To my long-time friend, Joan, who has tirelessly volunteered her
time to help proof the recipe ingredients as well as listened
patiently to my joy and frustration.
We have laughed hilariously and sometimes nearly cried trying to
decipher handwriting and meanings of many of the recipe
ingredients and directions.
A special thank you to my sons, Mark, Gary and John
and their families for their love and support!

Introduction

I have cooked for my family for many years and, like most cooks, have accumulated slips of paper, clippings from cans and magazines as well as a supply of good and bad recipe books. I hosted a cooking program on the local AM radio station for 2 years in the early 2000's and so many listeners were kind enough to send recipes and/or appear as an in-person guest on my program. Many of these recipes are included in this collection. "Cooking" on the radio is a bit tricky but very inventive and requires a great deal of imagination. My guests ranged from members of my family, to school administrators, to a former governor and the current Vice President of the United States! He was running for a House seat at the time, but it's so exciting to see him in his Vice President role and know that we once sat in the same studio and discussed one of his wife's favorite recipes!

As I look back on my years of preparing food, even though at the time, I thought preparing dishes was difficult and time consuming, I am reminded of the difficulty they faced and the limited ingredients our ancestors had available in preparing their meals. This is just a few of them:

- Bacon, sausage, ham, lard, steaks, roasts, liver and ground meat weren't items to be purchased at the grocery as they are now. A hog and a beef must be fed and taken care of for several years before they could be butchered and processed into edible items. Meals with fresh meat were special during butchering time, but most of these meats were either smoked or canned to ensure they didn't go to waste.

- Chickens must be taken care of from young chicks, killed, plucked, cleaned thoroughly and cut up before they could grace the Sunday dinner table.

- Fresh eggs were not something that was offered at breakfast every day as we have become accustomed. They were used sparingly as ingredients in cakes and other dishes, but most of them were collected and sold or traded at the general store to enable folks to purchase staple items such as flour, sugar, salt and coffee.

- Fresh fruits and vegetables were plentiful in summer and fall months, however, many hours were spent processing and canning these items to ensure availability of them during the long winter months. Many fruits were turned into delicious jams and jellies. Some fruits and vegetables were also preserved by drying, either by stringing them on heavy thread and hanging them in a warm dry place or by spreading them on flat surfaces until they dried. Some were then reconstituted at a later time by soaking in water.

- Honey had to be cautiously gathered from the bee hives, which was a dangerous and sometimes deadly task if the gatherer was allergic to bee stings. However, it was a treasured item in most kitchens both as a sweetener for tea and coffee and as a recipe ingredient.

- Molasses was also used to sweeten many dishes. But it was, and still is, a time-consuming task to grind the juice from the sugar cane as it comes from the field. It must then be slow-cooked through many stages to end up as the thick, sweet molasses which were a staple in most households.

- Bread, rolls, corn bread, biscuits, pies, cakes and cookies were baked with great care and pride mostly by women. Today, they are readily available from groceries or bakeries and many men are proficient at baking these delicious items.

- Potatoes, cabbage, carrots, turnips and other root vegetables were stored in a cool basement or root cellar which was dug into the side of a hill. Vegetables were kept cool in the root cellar by a cool stream of water running through the floor of the cellar. Crocks of sauerkraut and pickles were also kept in these natural refrigerators.

- Milk certainly was not delivered daily by the milkman either! Cows needed to be milked twice daily. Milk was sometimes stored in jars placed in the cool stream running through the root cellar. Probably weekly, the cream of some milk was allowed to separate from the milk. The cream was then placed in a churn where it was plunged with a wooden "dasher" until the cream turned into wonderful rich butter. The milk left from the separation was termed "buttermilk" and was a great ingredient for baking.

- Snacks consisted of popcorn whose kernels were hand-shelled from a special corn grown in the garden or field. Homemade candies and other delicacies were special treats served mostly during the holidays.

- And, of course, until the 1930's electricity was not standard in most homes. This meant that food was cooked on a cook stove heated with wood or coal. Keeping a balanced oven temperature while baking on a wood or coal stove was a delicate chore and only experienced cooks could keep the oven at the proper temperature to ensure edible results. The person baking needed to be well versed in just how much or how little wood or coal needed to be added to maintain the correct temperature.

And so, we are very blessed to be able to go to the grocery, the meat market or the specialty shop to obtain necessary ingredients. Gas and electricity as well as a wide variety of sophisticated appliances are now available to allow the newest or most experienced cooks to make even the most involved recipes. It may seem cooking a simple meal for a family is time consuming and difficult but compared to the processes our ancestors had to follow just a few decades ago, we have it made!

You will notice in some instances several recipes for the same item have been included. This is due to the fact that many cooks made different versions of a dish, some with just a slight variance in ingredients or preparation. Also, some of the quantities of the ingredients may not be absolute since older and most times very good cooks did not use measuring spoons or cups but simply determined the quantities by feel or weight.

It has been a long and tiring experience to gather and enter these recipes into my computer. I have met so many interesting and enjoyable new friends and become reacquainted with old friends during this process. Many of these recipes are tried and tested to be delectable dishes, however, I have not prepared all of them. So, I cannot put my personal stamp of approval on the entire collection. I have been very particular about the source of the recipes that are included and endeavored to include ones that seemed desirable through a "cook's eye".

My desire is that experienced as well as new cooks or folks simply interested in reading recipes will enjoy those included in this collection. If they provide new ideas or recipes a person thought was lost forever, my purpose is satisfied!

Table of Content

Appetizers	11
Breads	23
Cakes	59
Candies	117
Casseroles	129
Cheesecakes	153
Cookies	157
Drinks	181
Jams & Jellies	187
Meat, Poultry & Seafood	191
Noodles & Dumplings	257
Other Desserts	271
Pies	291
Puddings	331
Salads	343
Sandwiches	371
Snacks	373
Soups	385
Vegetables	409
Index	432
Author Bio	443

APPETIZERS

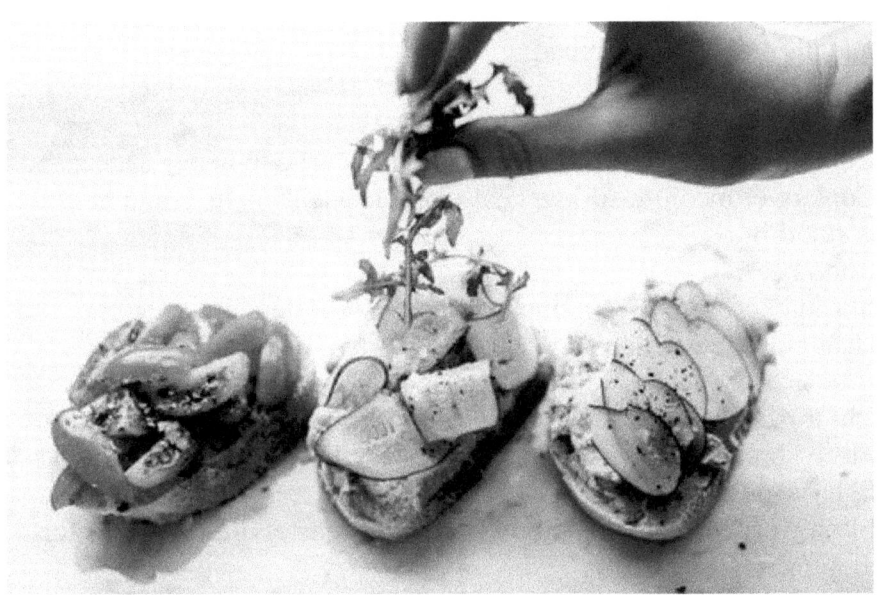

Chopped Beef Boule'
Bob Sparks

3 packages Carl Buddig Beef – 2.5 ounces each
½ cup milk
1 package cream cheese – 8 ounces
3 tablespoons green onion, chopped
1 clove garlic, minced
½ cup sour cream
1 tablespoon Dijon mustard
2 teaspoons Worcestershire sauce
1 loaf French Boule' bread

Combine milk, cream cheese, onion and garlic in heavy saucepan. Cook over medium-to-low heat until cheese is melted, and mixture is smooth.
Chop beef.
Stir in beef, sour cream, mustard and Worcestershire sauce.
Heat but do not boil.

Cut top off bread and cut out inside in pieces or strips.
Place "bread bowl" in oven and toast for 10-12 minutes or until light-to-golden brown.
Place warm dip in "bread bowl" and use toasted inside pieces for dipping.

Note: You can also use Roasted Garlic or Black Russian Rye bread for this "bread bowl".

Beef Cheese Ball
Linda Carson Ross

2 packages cream cheese, room temperature
1 container dried beef, chopped
½ teaspoon Worcestershire Sauce
Tops from small bundle of green onions, chopped

Combine all ingredients and form into a ball.
Chill.

Serve with your favorite crackers.

Gary's Cheese Ball
Gary Perkins

2 small packets cream cheese (Philadelphia Cream Cheese is far superior to other brands)
1 jar (2.25oz.) Armour dried beef.
4 green onions
4-6 dashes Worcestershire sauce
3-4 light shakes Accent flavor enhancer
Walnuts

Open cream cheese, place in large mixing bowl to warm.
Just allow cheese to warm enough to be workable.
Dice dried beef into approximately ½" squares.
Add to cream cheese.
Cut up green onions in ¼" rings.
Add to cheese.
Add Worcestershire sauce.
Add Accent - be careful with Accent; it can get too salty in a hurry!

Mix all ingredients well, by hand, and form ball.
Place walnuts in sandwich bag.
Fill bag approximately half full.
Use jar from dried beef to roll and crush walnuts finely.

Note: Save dried beef jar as a juice glass. You will soon have a full set!

Spread walnuts on large piece of aluminum foil.
Roll cheese ball in walnuts to cover.
Cover with aluminum foil and refrigerate until firm before serving.

Serve with Sociables and Chicken in a Biscuit crackers.

Beer Cheese Dip for Round Rye Bread
Hans Johansen, Jr.

1 lb. soft spreadable cheddar cheese
1 8-ounce package cream cheese
2 tablespoons soft margarine
½ tablespoon minced onion
1 pinch garlic salt
1 teaspoon hot pepper sauce
½ can beer, room temperature

Thoroughly mix all ingredients.
Cut circle out of top of round rye bread.
Dig bread out of the center making a bowl for the cheese dip.
Break removed bread into bite size pieces to be used for dipping and place on a platter around the "bowl" of bread.

Braunschweiger Ball
Hans Johansen, Jr.

Ball:

1 lb. Braunschweiger
1 small package dry onion soup mix
1 tablespoon hot water
1 tablespoon sugar
1 dash Tabasco sauce

Icing:

2 small packages of cream cheese with chives and onions, if available.
1 small package dry onion soup mix
1 tablespoon milk
1 tablespoon soft margarine
Garlic salt

Mix all ingredients together thoroughly including one of the small packages of onion soup mix.
Form into a ball and refrigerate to make firm.

Mix cream cheese, milk, margarine and one of the small packages of onion soup mix.
Ice the Braunschweiger ball using all of the icing, if possible.
Sprinkle with garlic salt.

Refrigerate until ready to serve.

Cheese Stuffed Mushrooms
Darla Huff Groves

1 large and 1 small package of white button mushrooms
2 packages vegetable blend Philadelphia cream cheese
1 stick butter, melted
1 large package Monterey Jack cheese, shredded
Garlic to taste

Clean and remove stems from mushrooms.
Cook in water approximately 5-10 minutes. Drain.
Fill each mushroom with cream cheese.
Add garlic to melted butter.
Pour in bottom of a 9"x13" baking pan.
Cover with shredded cheese.

Bake at 350 degrees for 30 minutes.

Cream Cheese Ball
Hans Johansen, Jr.

16-ounce package cream cheese
4 green onions, chopped
1 tablespoon Worcestershire sauce
1 teaspoon Accent seasoning
2 packages chipped beef, chopped

Chop onions and beef.
Reserve enough of the chopped beef for coating the ball.
Combine all ingredients and roll into a ball.
Roll ball in reserved chopped beef.

Refrigerate until ready to serve.

Ralph's Cocktail Sauce
Ralph Perkins

½ cup ketchup (Red Gold is best)
3-4 dashes Worcestershire sauce
1-2 dashes lemon juice
½ teaspoon pure prepared horseradish
Salt

Place ketchup in mixing bowl.
Add Worchester sauce and lemon juice.
Add horseradish.
Adjust amount of horseradish for taste. Horseradish varies by brand for taste and heat levels.
Add 2 pinches of salt.
Mix together and refrigerate to allow flavors to mix.

Wonderful with shrimp!

Tiropetas
Kitchen Aid Mixer Recipes

½ lb. feta cheese, drained and crumbled
1 3-ounce package cream cheese
½ cup cottage cheese
¼ cup grated Romano cheese
1/8 teaspoon pepper
Dash of nutmeg
2 eggs
1 lb. frozen prepared phyllo dough, thawed
1 cup butter or margarine, melted

Place feta cheese, cream cheese and cottage cheese in bowl.
Attach bowl and flat beater to mixer.
Turn to Speed 4 (medium) and beat until fluffy, about 1 minute.
Stop and scrape bowl.
Add Romano cheese, pepper and nutmeg.
Turn to Speed 2 (low) and beat 30 seconds.
Stop and scrape bowl.
Turn to Speed 2 (low) and add eggs, one at a time, beating 30 seconds after each addition.
Increase to Speed 4 (medium) and beat 15 seconds.

Place 1 sheet phyllo dough on a flat surface.
Cover remaining phyllo dough with a slightly damp towel.
Brush sheet with butter.
Cut lengthwise into strips, about 2-1/2 inches wide.
Place 1 teaspoon cheese mixture on a bottom corner of strip.
Fold over into a triangle shape and continue folding like a flag.
Brush with butter and place on greased baking sheet.
Repeat with remaining phyllo dough and cheese mixture.
Work quickly as phyllo dough dries out quickly.
Bake at 350 degrees until golden brown, about 15 to 20 minutes.
Serve immediately.

Yield: 16 servings (3 pieces per serving)

Warm Ruben Spread

Chef Rolf Meisterhans, Executive Chef
Columbia Club, Indianapolis

4 ounces cream cheese
½ cup Thousand Island dressing
¼ lb. sliced corned beef, chopped
¾ cup well drained sauerkraut
8 ounces sliced Swiss cheese, chopped
Rye Crackers or Wheat Crackers

Preheat oven to 350 degrees.
Mix the cream cheese and dressing in medium bowl.
Stir in all remaining ingredients except crackers.
Spread onto bottom of 9-inch pie plate or shallow dish.
Bake for 20 minutes or until heated through.
Serve warm with crackers.

Yield: 2-1/2 cups or 20 servings

Zucchini Appetizer
Dorcas Neidig

3 cups zucchini, sliced
1 cup Bisquick
½ cup chopped onion
½ cup grated Parmesan cheese
2 teaspoons parsley
½ teaspoon salt
1-1/2 teaspoons oregano
Pepper
1 clove garlic
1 cup grated cheddar cheese
½ cup oil
4 eggs

Combine all ingredients.
Bake in a greased 13x9 pan at 350 degrees for 35-40 minutes.
Serve warm or cold.

BREADS

Banana Bread
Versa Tolliver Smith

2 cups sifted flour
3 teaspoons baking powder
½ teaspoon salt
½ cup shortening
1 cup sugar
2 eggs, well beaten
1 cup dates, chopped
1 cup walnuts, chopped
1 cup mashed bananas
1 teaspoon lemon juice

Sift together flour, baking powder and salt and set aside.
Beat together shortening and sugar until light and fluffy.
Add beaten eggs, dates and walnuts.
Combine mashed bananas and lemon juice and add to mixture.
Add sifted dry ingredients.
Mix until well blended.
Turn into a greased and floured pan.

Bake at 350 degrees for 60-70 minutes.

Isabelle's Banana Bread
Hans Johansen, Jr.

2 cups flour
½ teaspoon baking powder
½ teaspoon baking soda
½ teaspoon salt
½ cup margarine, softened
1 cup sugar
2 eggs, slightly beaten
3 bananas, mashed
Nuts

Sift together flour, baking powder, soda and salt.
Add margarine, sugar, eggs, bananas and nuts.
Pour into greased and floured loaf pan.

Bake at 350 degrees for approximately 1 hour or until toothpick inserted comes out clean.

Aunt Ruby's Biscuits
Ruby Tolliver Brewster

2 cups flour
1-1/2 teaspoons baking powder
1 teaspoon salt
2 tablespoons shortening
Buttermilk or sweet milk

Combine flour, baking powder, salt and shortening.
Mix with fingers until mixture becomes small balls.
Add enough buttermilk or sweet milk to make soft dough.
Roll out on floured counter.
Cut with floured biscuit cutter or small glass.

Bake at 400 degrees until golden brown.

Bread
Edna Tolliver Hays Hollandsworth

1 package yeast
1-1/2 cups warm water
2 tablespoons sugar
1 teaspoon salt
4 tablespoons shortening
Flour

Dissolve yeast in warm water.
Add sugar, salt and shortening.
Add flour to make a stiff dough.

Grease dough with shortening and place in a greased bowl.
Let dough rise.
Punch dough down, put in a greased loaf pan and let rise again.

Bake at 325 degrees for 25 to 30 minutes or until golden brown.

Author's Note: Like the noodle recipes, each of the Tolliver cooks had their own special bread recipe. Whether they used regular flour or self-rising flour; dry yeast or rapid-rising yeast, you can be certain the result was delicious, mouth-watering goodness.

Cloud Bread
Helen Salyer Perkins Johansen

6 eggs
½ teaspoon cream of tartar
½ teaspoon salt
1 teaspoon sweetener
4 ounces cream cheese, very soft
1 capful vanilla

Separate eggs.
Beat egg whites and cream of tartar until very stiff. Set aside.
Beat egg yolks, salt, sweetener, cream cheese and vanilla.
Add ½ teaspoon cinnamon, if desired.
Gently combine egg yolk mixture and egg whites.
Scoop mixture onto cookie sheet covered with parchment paper, forming into 12 "buns".

Bake at 350 degrees for 25-30 minutes.

Corn Bread
Helen Salyer Perkins Johansen

Old Fashioned:

2 cups white or yellow corn meal - Stone ground meal is especially good!
2 cups buttermilk
1 teaspoon salt
1 teaspoon soda

Mix all ingredients well and pour into iron skillet that has been preheated in a 475-degree oven with approximately 1 teaspoon of bacon grease.
Bake at 450 degrees for about 30-45 minutes or until bread is brown on top.

Mom's Recipe:

2 cups corn meal
½ teaspoon salt
2 tablespoons baking powder
1/8 teaspoon soda
2 tablespoons cooking oil
1 cup (or more) buttermilk – enough to make a thin batter.

Mix all ingredients.
If you use self-rising corn meal, all you have to add is 1 egg, 2 tablespoons oil and buttermilk to mix.
Pour into skillet or pan sprayed with cooking spray (Pam).

Bake at 450 degrees for 30 minutes or so until bread is brown on top.

Better Homes & Gardens Corn Bread
Hans Johansen, Jr.

Dry Ingredients:

1 cup all-purpose flour
1 cup corn meal
¼ cup sugar (heaping)
1 tablespoon baking powder
½ teaspoon salt

Wet Ingredients:

2 eggs
1 cup milk
¼ cup oil

Combine dry ingredients and set aside.
Combine wet ingredients.
Add wet ingredients to dry ingredients.
Pour into 9x9 baking pan that has been sprayed with Pam.

Bake at 375 degrees for 20-25 minutes.

French Bread for Bread Machine
Hans Johansen, Jr.

2-1/4 cups water
3 teaspoons sugar
1-3/4 teaspoons salt
6 cups bread flour
1-1/2 tablespoons yeast

Combine all ingredients in bread machine container.
Mix on Dough cycle.
Turn out onto floured sheet or loaf pan.
Form into loaf shape of your choice – round, long or other.
Place in a warm location to rise for 45-60 minutes.
Brush water or egg white on top and sprinkle lightly with celery seed.

Bake in a 400-degree oven for 30 minutes or until medium brown on top.

Aunt Isabel's Ginger Bread
Hans Johansen, Jr.

1-1/2 sticks margarine, softened
1-1/2 cups brown sugar
3 whole eggs, well beaten
1-1/2 cups molasses
3-3/4 cups sifted all-purpose flour
1 teaspoon cinnamon
1 teaspoon ginger
1 cup boiling water
1 teaspoon soda

Combine margarine and brown sugar.
Add well beaten eggs.
Sift together flour, cinnamon and ginger.
Combine brown sugar/egg mixture and flour mixture.
Dissolve soda in boiling water and add to batter.

Pour into greased and floured 10" tube pan.

Bake at 350 degrees for one hour.

Test with a toothpick.

Cool, then loosen from pan with a sharp knife.

Light Bread
Willa Tolliver Salyer Lyons

2 packages yeast
3 tablespoons sugar
1 tablespoon salt
2 cups warm water
¼ cup oil
3 cups flour and more for kneading

In large bowl, measure 2 cups flour, yeast, salt, and sugar.
Mix well.
Add water and oil.
Beat well.
Add 1 cup flour and mix well.
Add enough flour to make a stiff dough.
Turn out on board or counter and knead about 10 minutes.
Place in greased bowl and let rise about 1 hour.
Punch down and put in greased loaf pans and let rise again.

Bake in hot oven – about 350 degrees – for 30-35 minutes until golden brown.

Aunt Nora's Donuts
Vicki Agner Yates

2 cups mashed potatoes
2 cups sugar
Butter – size of an egg
2 eggs
½ teaspoon salt
1 cup sweet milk
5 teaspoons baking powder
Flour

Mix warm mashed potatoes and sugar.
Add butter and mix until butter is melted.
Add beaten eggs, salt and baking powder and mix well.
Add milk and enough flour to be able to roll out on floured board.
Cut in desired shape.
Fry in hot oil.

Flavor to suit.

Quick Doughnuts
Edna Tolliver Hayes Hollandsworth

Take a can of 10 Ballard Oven-Ready Biscuits.
Cut a hole in center of each.
Deep fry the donuts and the balls from the center until golden brown.
Have ready a small dish of regular white sugar or sifted powdered sugar.
Drain donuts slightly as you take them out of the fryer.
Roll them over in the sugar.

Real Tasty!!

Elephant Ears

Ann Means
Classic Stained Glass & Gift Gallery
250 Hoosier Street
North Vernon, IN 47265
812-346-4527

1-1/2 cups milk
2 tablespoons sugar
1 teaspoon salt
6 tablespoons shortening
2 packets dry yeast
4 cups flour
Oil for frying
1 cup sugar
1 teaspoon cinnamon

Heat together milk, sugar, salt and shortening until shortening is melted – do not boil.
Cool to lukewarm.
Add yeast and stir until all yeast is dissolved.
Stir in flour, 2 cups at a time, beating until smooth after each addition.
Place in a greased bowl, cover with a damp cloth and let rise until double in size, about 30 minutes.

Dust hands with flour.
Pinch off pieces of dough about the size of a golf ball.
Stretch each ball into a thin 6-to-8 inch circle.
Have oil at 350 degrees.
Drop stretched dough, one at a time, into hot oil.

Elephant Ears (cont'd)

Fry until the elephant ear rises to the surface.
Turn and fry other side until light brown.
Drain well on paper towels.
Brush elephant ears with melted butter and then sprinkle cinnamon and sugar mixture over top.
The butter helps the sugar to adhere to the elephant ear.

Praline French Toast
Joan Neuenschwander Schug

8 large eggs, lightly beaten
1-1/2 cups half-and-half
1 tablespoon brown sugar
2 teaspoons vanilla extract
8 slices French bread, 1" thick

½ cup butter
¾ cup packed brown sugar
½ cup maple syrup
¾ cup chopped pecans (2-ounce package)

Combine first four ingredients in a large bowl.
Stir with a wire whisk until blended.
Pour 1 cup egg mixture into a greased 9x13 baking dish.
Place bread in dish.
Pour remaining egg mixture over bread.
Cover and chill 8 hours.

Preheat oven to 350 degrees.
Combine butter, brown sugar, maple syrup and pecans in microwave-safe bowl.
Cover with plastic wrap and microwave at HIGH setting for 30 seconds.
Pour over bread.

Bake uncovered for 30 minutes or until set and golden.

Funnel Cakes

Ann Means
Classic Stained Glass & Gift Gallery
250 Hoosier Street
North Vernon, IN 47265
812-346-4527

2 eggs
1-1/2 cups milk
2 cups flour
1 teaspoon baking powder
½ teaspoon salt
Vegetable oil for frying
Melted butter
1 cup sugar
1 teaspoon cinnamon
Powdered sugar

Mix flour, baking powder and salt and set aside.
Mix eggs and milk.
Add dry ingredients to eggs and milk.
Heat 1 inch of any vegetable oil for deep frying.
Heat to 375 degrees or until a 1-inch bread cube dropped in the oil browns in 45 seconds.

Pour ½ cup of batter into a medium funnel, holding your finger over the bottom of the funnel.
Hold over oil, remove finger and drop batter forming a circle, then criss-cross across the circle with batter.

Fry until golden brown, turning once.
Remove from pan and drain well on paper towels.

Brush top with melted butter.
Then sprinkle with sugar mixture (sugar and cinnamon).
Or sprinkle with powdered sugar the traditional way.

Hush Puppies
Willa Tolliver Salyer Lyons

2 eggs
1 cup buttermilk
3 tablespoons margarine, melted
1 cup corn meal
1 cup flour
1 onion, diced
¼ teaspoon garlic powder
½ teaspoon baking soda
½ teaspoon salt

Whisk buttermilk, margarine and eggs in a bowl.
Combine corn meal, flour, baking soda and salt in a separate bowl.
Fold in buttermilk mixture and onion just until mixed.
Drop by tablespoon into oil in Fry Baby or hot oil in a heavy saucepan a few at a time so they aren't crowded in the oil.
Fry until golden brown, turning to cook evenly, about 6-10 minutes.
Remove hush puppies with a slotted spoon and place on paper towels to drain.

Keep warm in a low-heat oven until ready to serve.

Hush Puppies
Ruby Brady (Mrs. Leck) Tolliver

2 eggs, well beaten
1 teaspoon salt
2 teaspoons sugar
1/2 teaspoon baking soda
1 cup buttermilk
1 1/2 cups corn meal
1/2 cup flour
1/4 cup onion, minced
1 tablespoon fat (oil, Crisco, etc.)

Combine all ingredients.
Shape into balls.

Drop into fat heated to 365 degrees.

Author's Note: Daughter Wanda said her Mommie's hush puppies were the best. Her Mom loved to fish but the only thing she loved more than fishing was cooking up a fish feast. She always made her delicious hush puppies to go with the fish. Not from a mix; always from scratch with those tiny pieces of fresh onion in them.

Cranberry Almond Muffins
Judy Kiel McKain

1 can jellied whole cranberry sauce
2 cups flour
¾ cup granulated sugar
1-1/2 teaspoons baking powder
½ teaspoon baking soda
½ teaspoon salt
3 eggs
6 tablespoons butter, melted
¾ cup sour cream
1 teaspoon almond extract
1 cup chopped almonds
½ cup dried cranberries

Place cranberry sauce in a strainer; rinse with warm water and set aside to drain.

Combine flour, sugar, baking powder, baking soda and salt in a large bowl.

In another bowl, whisk eggs, butter, sour cream and almond extract; add to dry ingredients and mix thoroughly.
Mix in ½ cup of almonds, cranberries and cranberry sauce.
Fill paper-lined muffin cups; sprinkle with remaining almonds.
Bake at 375 degrees for 20-25 minutes. Wait 10 minutes before removing from pan.

Yield: One dozen muffins

Note: This recipe was shared by my daughter, Liz Tuecke. She loved following me in the kitchen from a very young age and was baking on her own by the age of 8. She was good with her fractions and had no trouble doubling her recipes.

Popovers
Hans Johansen, Jr.

1 cup sifted all-purpose flour
½ teaspoon salt
2 large eggs
1 cup milk
Melted unsalted butter for brushing the popover pan

In a bowl, sift together flour and salt.
In a small bowl, whisk together eggs and milk.
Add the milk mixture to the flour mixture, stirring until the batter is smooth.
In a preheated 450-degree oven, heat a six-cup popover pan, a muffin pan or six 2/3-cup custard cups for 5 minutes.
Brush the cups with the melted butter.
Fill them half full with batter.

Bake the popovers on the middle rack of a 450-degree oven for 20 minutes.

Reduce heat to 375 degrees and bake the popovers for 20 minutes more or until they are golden brown and crisp.

Note: Popovers are delicious when sliced or broken open and filled with butter and jelly or apple butter!

Aunt Ruby's Yeast Rolls
Ruby Tolliver Brewster

2 packages cake or dry yeast
2 cups warm water (not hot)
3 tablespoons oil
1 tablespoon salt
1/3 cup sugar
5-6 cups flour (Gold Medal or Pillsbury)

Dissolve yeast in warm water.
Add oil, salt, sugar and flour.
Stir until smooth and stiff.
Cover dough and allow to rise in warm area until doubled in size.
Work down dough and roll into balls.
Place balls in greased pan and flatten a bit on top.
Allow dough balls to rise until doubled in size again.
Brush top of balls with butter before and after baking.

Bake at 400 degrees for approximately 20 minutes or until golden brown.

Recipe can also be baked in bread pans.

Homemade Yeast Rolls
(Makes 4 loaves of bread.)
Versa Tolliver Smith

1 teaspoon sugar
5 cups warm water
4 tablespoons sugar
1 package dry yeast
4 teaspoons salt
2 cups all-purpose flour
4 tablespoons shortening, melted

Dissolve sugar in 1 cup of lukewarm water.
Stir in package of dry yeast.
Let sit 5 minutes.
Put into large bowl.
Add 4 cups warm water, salt and melted shortening.

Stir in enough flour to make very stiff dough.
When stiff enough to handle, turn out onto floured board.
Knead in as much flour as dough can take without becoming ragged.

Put into large, greased container to raise until double.
Work down and shape into rolls or loaves.
Put into greased pans.
Let double.

Bake in oven at 350 degrees until golden brown on top.
Grease tops with shortening or butter.
Turn out immediately onto clean dry cloth and cover.

Author's Note: Aunt Versa's grandson, Mark Wical, shared the following memories:

I remember Uncle Roger would come to visit us and he would ask Mom (Opal Louise Wical) to bake him some homemade bread, and he paid her $1 a loaf just to get some. Nobody in the family could bake homemade light bread like my Mom. They all tried but could never quite get it right. I used to watch her make it all the time. I was fascinated with the process, and the reward after it was done made the cleanup well worth it. I remember my first batch. I baked some homemade buns, and took some to Mom and Dad. Mom's jaw dropped when I brought them in all hot and smelling good. After she ate them, she said, "You've got the knack." It was a proud moment for me to say the least. I remember her talking to Aunt Phyllis, saying that they were better than hers (as a mother I think she had to say that). We looked forward to Thanksgiving and Christmas every year because Mom would make homemade buns and noodles and pies. Her butterscotch pie was to die for and she only made it for Christmas most of the time. After my brother and I were grown up and gone, we would go there on Christmas Eve, and she would have butterscotch pie for me and chocolate pie for my brother. Good times!

Mamaw's Rolls
Danni Burgmeier Malcomb

9 cups flour
1 cup sugar
1 cup shortening
1 12-ounce can evaporated milk
2 packages yeast
2-1/2 cups warm water
1 teaspoon baking soda
2 teaspoons baking powder
1 tablespoon salt

Preheat oven to 400 degrees.

Mix yeast and ½ cup warm water in a small bowl. (Water must be warm enough to activate the yeast but not so hot it will kill it. Between 120-130 degrees.) Set aside.

Melt shortening in a large bowl. Stir and add sugar.

Mix evaporated milk and water in a measuring cup to make a total of 4 cups liquid.

Add milk and water mix to shortening and sugar. Heat and stir until mixture is liquid. (DO NOT exceed a temperature that will kill the yeast.)

Add yeast mixture to mixture in large bowl. Stir.

Add 8 cups flour, one cup at a time. Mix well. Cover and allow to rise in a warm place for one hour or until double in size.

Sift 1 cup flour, baking powder, baking soda and salt into a small bowl. Set aside. <u>Once dough has risen,</u> punch down and add this mixture to it.

Mamaw's Rolls (cont'd)

Roll dough on floured surface to about ½ inch thickness. Use biscuit cutter to cut dough.
Lay cuts side by side on a cookie sheet. Place a pea sized chunk of butter in the middle of each. Fold in half, pinching the middle of the edge to hold roll shut.

Bake 15-20 minutes.

Note: This I the roll recipe from my Great Grandma, Nerissa (Clark) Boling of Sevierville, Tennessee; born September 16, 1898. I have no idea how old the recipe actually is, but I imagine it was passed down for many generations. My Grandma, Lythia (Boling) Armbrister, is the person that taught me how to make these. THEY ARE DELICIOUS!

Sausage Muffins
Helen Salyer Perkins

1 cup Bisquick
1 lb. cooked sausage
4 eggs, beaten
1 cup shredded cheddar

Combine all ingredients.
Pour into greased muffin pan.

Bake at 350 degrees for 20 minutes.

Mom's Southern Spoon Bread
Hans Johansen, Jr.

2 cups white corn meal
2 cups boiling water
1 teaspoon salt
3 tablespoons butter, melted
1-1/2 cups milk
3 whole eggs, separated

Beat egg whites until stiff.
Add meal to boiling water.
Add salt, butter, milk and egg yolks, lightly beaten.
Fold in beaten egg whites.

Pour into greased baking dish.

Bake at 350 degrees for 45 minutes.

Southern Spoon Bread
Joyce Perkins Purnell

1 cup plain corn meal
2 cups boiling milk
2 tablespoons cooking oil or melted butter
1 teaspoon salt
1 teaspoon baking powder
1 cup cold milk
3 eggs, separated

In a saucepan, pour meal into boiling milk.
Cook approximately 2 minutes until the consistency of mush.
Cool.
Add salt, baking powder, butter or oil, and cold milk.
Add well-beaten egg yolks.
Fold in stiffly beaten egg whites.

Bake in greased 2-quart baking dish at 325 degrees for about 1 hour.

Spoon onto plates while hot.
Top with butter.

Quick Sweet Rolls
Mary Keller

1 can biscuits (cheap ones work best)
¼ cup butter or margarine
1/3 to ½ cup brown sugar, packed
Chopped nuts – pecans or walnuts

Melt butter in an 8-inch round cake pan.
Sprinkle brown sugar evenly over butter.
Add the amount of nuts to your taste.
Raisins can also be used – to your taste.
Place biscuits over the top.

Bake at 375 degrees until brown.
Remove from oven and turn upside down on plate.
Remove pan.
Enjoy!!

Note: You can sprinkle cinnamon over the butter and sugar for a change.

Mom's Easter Tea Ring
Dorcas Neidig

1-1/2 cups milk, scalded
2 packages yeast
½ cup sugar
3 eggs, beaten
2 teaspoons salt
5 cups flour
½ cup margarine, melted

Topping:
½ cup brown sugar
1 teaspoon cinnamon
½ cup pecans, chopped

Cool scalded milk to warm, then add yeast.
Stir until dissolved.
Add sugar, eggs, salt and flour.
Mix well.

Add cooled melted butter and mix thoroughly.
Turn onto floured board and knead until dough is smooth and elastic, working in additional flour if necessary, to prevent stickiness.

Place dough in bowl, brush with oil or fat, and let rise until doubled in bulk.
Divide dough into 2 or 3 balls.
Roll into oblong shape.

Brush with 1 tablespoon melted butter and sprinkle with topping mixture.

Mom's Easter Tea Ring (cont'd)

Join the ends to form a ring.
Cut with scissors from outer part toward center.
Shape slices by pulling out and lapping one over the other.
Bake at 350 degrees for 30 minutes.
Ice with butter icing and sprinkle with nuts.

Angel Waffles
Judy Kiel McKain

1 cup butter, softened (2 sticks)
2 cups buttermilk
2 cups flour
4 eggs, well beaten
1 teaspoon baking soda
3 teaspoons baking powder

Mix dry ingredients.

Add butter, buttermilk and eggs.

Mix well and bake in waffle iron according to the directions with the waffle iron.

Serve hot with butter and your choice of syrup.

Top with whipped cream and fruit, if desired.

Note: My mother, the late Ada Pearl Eble, would often stir up a batch of these fluffy waffles along with sausage patties or bacon to serve Sunday afternoon guests who dropped by and stayed until supper time. She had the gift of hospitality and was always happy to accommodate family and friends. This recipe continues to be a favorite even to the third generation.

Delicious Yeast Rolls
Ollie Carter Purnell

2 packages yeast
1 teaspoon sugar
¼ cup warm water
2 eggs, beaten
½ cup sugar
½ cup shortening
2 cups boiled water (cooled)
1 tablespoon salt
8 cups flour

In small bowl, mix yeast, 1 teaspoon sugar and warm water.
In large bowl, mix eggs, ½ cup sugar, shortening, cooled water and salt.
Stir in yeast mixture.
Add 4 cups flour.
Mix and beat until elastic.
Add 4 more cups of flour.
Knead until smooth.
Put in a greased large bowl and set in a warm place covered.
Let rise until doubled in size.
Punch down.
Shape into rolls and put into greased pans.
Cover and let rise in a warm place until doubled in size.

Bake at 425 degrees for 15-20 minutes or until golden brown.
May brush tops with butter after baking.

Note: If using bulk yeast, 1 scant tablespoon is the same as 1 package of yeast.

Good Waffles
Edna Tolliver Hayes Hollandsworth

1-1/3 cups flour
½ teaspoon salt
2 teaspoons baking powder
2 eggs
1 teaspoon sugar
¼ cup butter or margarine, melted
1 cup sweet milk

Sift flour and measure.
Sift flour with salt and baking powder.
Add sugar and shortening.
Mix well.
Add milk alternately with sifted dry ingredients.
Fold in well-beaten eggs.
Bake on hot (oiled) waffle iron.

Serve while hot with melted butter or substitute and syrup or honey.

Makes 6 servings

Opal's Zucchini Bread
Willa Tolliver Salyer Lyons

3 large eggs
1 cup oil
2 cups sugar
2 cups zucchini, shredded
2 teaspoons vanilla
3 cups flour
1 teaspoon salt
1 teaspoon baking soda
1 teaspoon baking powder
1 tablespoon cinnamon
½ teaspoon cloves
1-1/2 teaspoons allspice
1 cup raisins
¾ cup nuts

Beat eggs until light and foamy.
Add oil and sugar.
Beat well.
Stir in zucchini.
Sift flour, salt, baking soda, baking powder and spices.
Add to zucchini mixture.
Stir in raisins and nuts.
Pour equal parts into 2 loaf pans, greased and floured.

Bake at 300 degrees for 1 hour.

CAKES

Apple Cake
Julie Oreson Perkins

4 cups uncooked apples
1-1/2 cups sugar
2 teaspoons baking powder
2 cups flour
4 teaspoons cinnamon
1 teaspoon salt
2 unbeaten eggs
¾ cup vegetable oil

Peel apples and chop into chunks.
Any kind of apples, but baking apples or red delicious are good. Sugar can be decreased a bit if you don't want it so sweet or increased a bit if you're using more "sour" or "tart" apples.
Mix all ingredients with a spoon until less granular and more "liquid" or "soupy" or "stew like."

Note: Don't mix the ingredients until you have everything in the bowl. At first, it won't look like it could possibly turn out "soupy" but it does!

Pour into ungreased 9x13 glass baking dish.

Bake at 350 degrees for 50-60 minutes.

Test for doneness like you would a regular cake by inserting a toothpick in the center. If it comes out clean, the cake is done.

Apple Cake (cont'd)

This dish is great with fresh Fall baking apples and is perfect for dessert with vanilla ice cream. It's even been served warm as part of a breakfast buffet.

Enjoy!

History: As far as I know, this recipe is from an unnamed family restaurant in the Northeast. The story goes that a waitress there, at the request of the customers, had been asking the owner/chef for the recipe but he wouldn't give it up. So, over time, she gleaned the ingredients/recipe as he made it and then she passed the recipe on. My Mother, then a school teacher, first experienced this apple cake at a school function, then she got the recipe, then I got the recipe and so on……

All I ask is that as you enjoy this easy, tasty Apple Cake recipe, give thanks to the unknown creator of this delicious treat! THANK YOU!

Apple Sauce Cake
Ollie Carter Purnell (submitted by Vicki Agner Yates)

2-3/4 cups flour
2 cups sugar
¼ teaspoon baking powder
1-1/2 teaspoons soda
1-1/2 teaspoons salt
¾ teaspoon cinnamon
½ teaspoon cloves
½ teaspoon allspice
½ cup shortening
½ cup water
1-1/2 cups apple sauce
2 eggs, beaten
1 cup raisins
½ cup chopped nuts

Combine first eight dry ingredients.
Add shortening.
Mix water and apple sauce.
Beat two minutes.
Add beaten eggs.
Stir in raisins and nuts.

Pour batter into a greased and floured pan.

Bake at 350 degrees for 40 minutes.
Allow cake to cool for 15 minutes, then turn out onto serving plate.

Serve warm.

Blackberry Cake

Opal Tolliver Bowles Ruble

2-1/2 cups flour
2 cups sugar
2 teaspoons baking soda
½ teaspoon salt
1 teaspoon cinnamon
½ teaspoon allspice
½ teaspoon cloves
¼ teaspoon nutmeg
½ cup vegetable oil
3 eggs
1 cup blackberry juice, unsweetened
1 teaspoon vanilla
1 cup blackberries, well drained
½ cup nuts, chopped (optional)

Combine all ingredients in bowl except for blackberries and nuts.
Mix well.
Stir in nuts and berries.
Bake at 350 degrees for 25 to 30 minutes in two 9-inch cake pans.
Cool.

Caramel Icing

1 stick butter or margarine, melted
1 cup brown sugar, packed
¼ cup milk
Powdered sugar

Combine margarine and brown sugar and stir continuously over medium heat until it bubbles.
Add milk.
Then cook, stirring until it bubbles.

Blackberry Cake (cont'd)

Cook one minute more.
Remove from heat and let cool.
Add powdered sugar until desired texture.

Author's Note: Son Cary remembers his Mom's fantastic blackberry cake was always the best, however, he liked it most with no icing, so his Mom would always make some special cake for him without icing. His wife, Linda, makes the cake without icing for him now. Cary said the cake seemed even better when his Mom made it with fresh berries.

One of Cary's wildest memories of the cake was when they were traveling to the Tolliver reunion. His Dad loved to take a short cut across Hackleshin Road. The rough road caused all the items stacked along the back window of the car to come flying down! Luckily, his sister Lou Ellen's head saved the cake cover and the blackberry cake inside from damage. However, Lou Ellen wasn't too happy.

Blackberry Cake with Coffee
Ollie Carter Purnell

1-1/2 cups sugar
½ cup shortening
2 eggs, beaten
1 cup strong coffee
2 cups flour
2 teaspoons soda
1 teaspoon baking powder
1 teaspoon cloves
3 tablespoons cocoa
2 teaspoons cinnamon
1 teaspoon vanilla
1 cup canned blackberries, drained

Combine sugar and shortening.
Add beaten eggs and mix well.
Combine flour, soda, baking powder, cloves, cocoa and cinnamon.
Add to sugar, shortening and egg mixture.
Add vanilla and blackberries.
Pour into three 9-inch cake pans.

Bake at 350 degrees for 25-30 minutes or until toothpick comes out clean.

Note: Blackberry jam can be used in place of the canned blackberries. If using jam, omit ½ cup of the sugar.

Blackberry Cake with Coffee (cont'd)

Caramel Icing:

2 cups light brown sugar
½ cup butter
½ cup cream
1 teaspoon vanilla

Combine sugar, butter and cream in a heavy skillet or pan.
Place on low heat and mix until smooth.
Bring slowly to a boil.
Boil until thick and waxy. (Soft ball on candy thermometer.)

Take from heat and add vanilla.
Stir and beat until thick enough to spread.
It remains soft and delicious to the last bite!

Brato Cake or Hawaiian Cake
Carolyn Poling

2 cups sifted flour
2 cups sugar
2 teaspoons vanilla
2 teaspoons baking soda
2 eggs
1 can crushed pineapple with juice
1 cup walnuts, chopped
1 banana, smashed

Mix all ingredient together by hand.
Pour into a greased and floured 9" x 13" cake pan.
Bake at 350 degrees for 35 to 40 minutes.

Frosting

2 teaspoons vanilla
8 ounces cream cheese
1 cup walnuts, chopped
3 cups powdered sugar
1 stick butter

Mix together cream cheese and butter with a mixer until creamy.
Add rest of the ingredients and mix together.
Put on warm cake.

Brownie Supreme

Mary Etta Roth
Grateful Grubb Family Restaurant
412 South Madison Avenue
North Vernon, IN 47265
812-346-0004

2 boxes brownie mix
1 extra large egg
1 8-ounce package cream cheese, softened
1 cup powdered sugar
2 8-ounce containers whipped topping
1 3-ounce package instant chocolate pudding
1 3-ounce package instant vanilla pudding
3-1/2 cups milk
1 Hershey candy bar or chocolate syrup

Mix brownie mixes according to package directions.
Add 1 extra egg.
Bake in a 9x13 greased and floured cake pan.
Mix cream cheese, powdered sugar and 1 container whipped topping.
Spread this mix on top of the cooled brownies.
Blend puddings and milk together and put on top of the cream cheese mixture.
Top with another layer of whipped topping.
Put chocolate shavings or swirl chocolate syrup on top.
Refrigerate until ready to serve.

Carrot Cake

Greg & Kim Evans
Crossroads Family Restaurant & Gift Shop
615 West Highway 50
Versailles, IN 47042

2-1/2 cups sugar
½ cup brown sugar
6 eggs, lightly beaten
2 cups oil
2 teaspoons vanilla
3 cups flour
2 teaspoons baking powder
1-1/2 teaspoons salt
½ 12-ounce can crushed pineapple
2 teaspoons cinnamon
3 cups carrots, grated
1-1/2 cups pecans

Mix all ingredients.
Divide into 3 round cake pans.
Bake for 27 minutes at 325 degrees.
Remove from pans and let cool.

Cream Cheese Icing

4 packages cream cheese, softened
1 stick salted butter, softened
Vanilla
Powdered sugar

Combine cream cheese and butter.
Add vanilla to taste.
Add powdered sugar until icing is spreading consistency.

Chocolate Éclair Cake
Lori Tolliver Holberg

1 box graham crackers (3 packages)
2 small boxes Instant French Vanilla or Banana Cream pudding mix
3-1/2 cups milk
1 8-ounce tub Cool Whip

Butter bottom of 9x13 pan.
Line pan with whole graham crackers.
Combine pudding mix and milk.
Blend in Cool Whip.
Pour ½ of pudding mixture over graham crackers.
Add another layer of graham crackers.
Pour remainder of mixture over graham crackers.
Top with graham crackers.
Refrigerate for 2 hours or overnight.

Topping:

3 chocolate squares, melted
3 teaspoons white corn syrup
3 teaspoons vanilla
3 tablespoons butter
2 cups powdered sugar
4 tablespoons milk

Combine chocolate squares, corn syrup, vanilla and butter.
Add powdered sugar.
Add milk – more or less until desired consistency for spreading.
Spread over crackers and refrigerate for 2 more hours.

Marbaugh Chocolate Cake
John and Sara Marbaugh

1-1/4 cups sugar
1 cup Miracle Whip (not light!)
4-5 tablespoons baking cocoa
1 teaspoon vanilla
2 cups flour
2 teaspoons baking soda dissolved in 1cup of water

Preheat oven to 350 degrees.

Grease, but do NOT flour 2 round cake pans.
Combine above ingredients and divide evenly into cake pans.
Bake at 350 degrees for 25 minutes.
Use toothpicks to test for doneness.

Frosting:

½ cup (1 stick) butter
2/3 cup Hershey's Cocoa
3 cups powdered sugar
1/3 cup milk
1 teaspoon vanilla

Melt butter.
Stir in cocoa.
Alternately add powdered sugar and milk, beating to spreading consistency.
Stir in vanilla.
To test consistency: Draw into peaks with a spoon; if it stays upright without being too stiff, then it's good!
Add small amounts of additional milk or powdered sugar, if needed.

Makes about 2 cups

Chocolate Skillet Cake with Peanut Butter and Chocolate Icing
Susan Matthews Wisecup

1 cup flour
½ teaspoon baking soda
1 cup sugar
¼ teaspoon salt
¼ cup (1/2 stick) butter
¼ cup vegetable oil
2 tablespoons cocoa powder
½ cup water
¼ cup buttermilk
1 egg
½ teaspoon vanilla

Preheat oven to 350 degrees.
In a large bowl, whisk together flour, baking soda, sugar and salt. Set aside.
In a 10-inch cast iron skillet, bring the butter, vegetable oil, cocoa powder and water to a boil.
Remove from heat and begin to whisk in the dry ingredients.
Next, with a spatula, incorporate the buttermilk, egg and vanilla until just combined.
Bake for 20-25 minutes or until a toothpick inserted near the center comes out clean.

Icing:
¼ cup (1/2 stick) butter
2 tablespoons cocoa
4-5 tablespoons milk (more, if needed)
½ cup peanut butter
2 cups powdered sugar
½ teaspoon vanilla
Ice cream for serving, optional

Chocolate Skillet Cake (cont'd)

While the cake begins to cool, prepare the icing.
In a saucepan, bring the butter, cocoa and milk to a boil.
Remove the pan from the heat and stir in the peanut butter.
Next, add the powdered sugar and vanilla.
Mix until smooth.
Depending on the consistency, add more milk, one tablespoon at a time, until the icing is just pourable but not runny.
Pour over the warm cake and smooth out with a spatula.

Allow the icing to set before serving with vanilla ice cream.

Note: Recipe was found by Susan on Pinterest on inspiredbycharm.com.

Caramel Frosted Apple Cake
Derek Holliday

4-1/2 cups fresh apples, peeled and chopped
2 eggs, beaten
1-1/2 cups vegetable oil
1-3/4 cups all-purpose flour
2 teaspoons baking powder
1 teaspoon baking soda
1 teaspoon salt
1 teaspoon cinnamon
½ teaspoon nutmeg
¼ teaspoon allspice
1-1/2 cups chopped nuts

In a large mixing bowl, beat eggs.
Add oil and sugar.
Beat until smooth and creamy.
Sift together flour, baking powder, baking soda, salt, cinnamon, nutmeg and allspice.
Gradually stir into egg, oil and sugar mixture. Batter will be stiff.
Add vanilla, apples and nuts.
Stir gently to mix thoroughly.
Place in greased and floured 9x13 baking dish.
Bake at 350 degrees for 50-55 minutes or until done.
Cool completely and frost with Caramel Frosting.

Caramel Frosting:

½ cup butter or margarine
1 cup brown sugar, firmly packed
1/8 teaspoon salt
¼ cup milk
1-3/4 to 2 cups powdered sugar

Caramel Frosted Apple Cake (cont'd)

Melt butter or margarine in heavy saucepan.
Add brown sugar and salt; stir well.
Bring to a boil over low heat.
Boil two minutes, stirring constantly.
Add milk (2% can be used, but whole milk makes better frosting).
Continue stirring until mixture comes to a boil.
Remove from heat.
Cool for 20 minutes.
Add powdered sugar a little at a time, beating well after each addition.
Beat until thick enough to frost cake.
If any frosting is left, add another ½ cup or so of powdered sugar and pour onto buttered saucer.
Makes great fudge!!

Chocolate Sundae Cake
Dorcas Neidig

20-25 Oreo cookies, crushed
¼ cup melted butter
½ gallon vanilla ice cream
1 16-ounce can Hershey's syrup
1 12-ounce container Cool Whip
½ cup chopped nuts

Mix Oreo cookies and melted butter.
Press into 9x13 inch pan and freeze.
Layer ice cream over cookies.
Pour can of Hershey's syrup over ice cream and refreeze.
Spread Cool Whip on top and sprinkle with crushed Oreos and nuts.

Keep frozen until ready to serve.

Opal Tolliver's Cinnamon Bread (Cake)
Opal Tolliver Bowles Ruble

1-1/2 cups sifted flour
1 cup sugar
2 teaspoons cinnamon
2 teaspoons baking powder
¼ teaspoon salt
¼ cup butter, melted
¾ cup milk
1 egg

Combine dry ingredients.
Add egg and milk and beat well.
Add melted butter and beat well
Pour into greased and floured pan.
Bake at 350 degrees until toothpick or broom straw comes out clean.

May put icing on top as desired (white, chocolate etc.)

Note: Opal's daughter, Lou Ellen Bowles Wilson, said she learned to make this bread (cake) as a teenager. It always turned out great! My brothers, Cary & Tony, and I really enjoyed this treat!

Dump Cake
Vicki Agner Yates

1 can cherry pie filling
1 can crushed pineapple
1 box yellow cake mix
1 stick butter, melted
1 package shredded coconut
1 cup chopped pecans

Pour pie filling in bottom of a 9x13 pan.
Spread crushed pineapple on top of pie filling.
Spread dry cake mix evenly over pineapple.
Pour melted butter over cake mix in a zig-zag pattern.
Sprinkle coconut and pecans on top.

Bake at 350-degrees for 1 hour.

Fresh Orange Pound Cake
Joyce Bessenger

6 medium oranges
1-3/4 cups sugar
1 cup margarine or butter, softened
3 cups all-purpose flour
1 teaspoon baking powder
¾ teaspoon vanilla
½ teaspoon baking soda
¼ teaspoon salt
4 large eggs
Powdered sugar for garnish

Preheat oven to 350 degrees.
Grease and flour 10-inch Bundt pan or tube pan.
Grate 2 tablespoons of zest from oranges and squeeze 1 cup juice.
In large bowl, with mixer at high speed, beat sugar and margarine or butter until light and fluffy, about 10 minutes.
Add flour, baking powder, vanilla, baking soda, salt, eggs and orange juice.
Beat at low speed until well mixed, constantly scraping bowl with rubber spatula.
Increase speed to medium and beat mixture 2 minutes, occasionally scraping bowl with rubber spatula.
Blend in grated orange zest.
Spoon batter into pan.
Bake 55 minutes or until toothpick inserted in center of cake comes out clean.
Cool cake in pan on wire rack 15 minutes.
Remove from pan and cool completely on rack.
Dust cake with powdered sugar.

Friendship Cake
Joyce Perkins Purnell

On the first day, in a wide-mouthed gallon container, mix together:
1-1/2 cup starter *
2-1/2 cups sugar
1 can sliced peaches with juice

Stir daily for 10 days.

On the 10th day, add:
2-1/2 cups sugar
1 large can pineapple chunks, with juice

Stir daily for 10 days.

On the 20th day, add:
2 9-ounce jars maraschino cherries, drained

Stir daily for 10 days.

On the 30th day:
Drain fruit and blend fruit in a blender.
Save juice as this is starter for your friends.
Makes four 1-1/2 cups of starter.

For one cake (Mix each cake separately):

1-1/2 cups blended fruit
1 cup chopped pecans or black walnuts
4 eggs
1 box white or yellow cake mix
2/3 cup Crisco oil
1 box vanilla instant pudding

Mix well and pour into greased and floured tube cake pan.

Friendship Cake (cont'd)

Bake at 350 degrees for 1 hour.

May ice cake but it is delicious with Cool Whip.
Cakes freeze well not iced.
Refrigerate starter if not used same day; will keep 3 days.

Good eating!!

Note: It takes 30 days to prepare the fruit for this cake, but it's worth it. If you are lucky, a friend will give you 2 cups of starter along with a piece of cake, so you won't have to go to all the trouble of preparing a starter. It will actually take 50 days total if you need to make the starter.

To make your own starter: *

1 15-ounce can pineapple chunks, drained
1 15-ounce can apricot halves, drained
1 15-ounce can sliced peaches, drained
1 10-ounce jar maraschino cherries, drained
1-1/4 cups brandy
1-1/4 cups white sugar

In a large glass jar, combine drained pineapple chunks, drained apricot halves, drained sliced peaches, drained maraschino cherries, brandy and sugar.
Stir gently with wooden spoon.
Cover and let stand at room temperature for 3 weeks, stirring at least twice a week.
Drain and reserve the liquid.
This liquid is your starter for the Thirty Day Friendship Cake.

Note: The brandied fruit should be kept refrigerated and can be served with ice cream, yogurt or pound cake.

Fruit Cocktail Salad Cake
Ruby Tolliver Brewster

1-1/2 cups sugar
2 teaspoons soda
2 cups flour
2 eggs
Juice poured off of 2 cups fruit cocktail
2 cups fruit cocktail
1 cup coconut
½ cup brown sugar

Combine sugar, soda and flour.
Mix well.
Add eggs and fruit cocktail juice.
Mix well.
Add fruit cocktail.
Mix well.

In a separate bowl, combine coconut and brown sugar.
Mix well.
Pour batter into a floured and greased cake pan.
Sprinkle coconut mixture over batter.
Bake at 350 degrees for 35-40 minutes.

While cake is baking, mix:
1-1/2 cups sugar
1 cup canned milk
¾ cup margarine
2 teaspoons vanilla

Bring to a boil.
Pour over cake while cake is still hot.
Will run to sides of cake.
Take a spoon and spoon mixture towards middle of cake until it all sinks in.

Fruit Cake
Willa Tolliver Salyer Lyons

2/3 cup shortening
1-1/2 cups sugar
1-1/2 cups boiling water
2 cups dates, chopped
1 cup raisins
2 teaspoons baking soda
½ teaspoon salt
2 teaspoons cinnamon
1 teaspoon cloves
1 teaspoon nutmeg
4 eggs
3 cups flour
1 cup nuts, chopped
English walnut halves
Red and green maraschino cherries, cut in half
Honey

Pour boiling water over dates and raisins; let stand 5 minutes.
Mix dry ingredients.
Add shortening.
Beat eggs.
Add eggs, nuts, and dates and raisins (with liquid).

Bake in greased tube pan or two (2) loaf pans at 300 degrees for 1-1/2 hours or until a straw placed in the center of the cake comes out clean. If baked in loaf pans, check doneness after 1 hour.

While cake is warm, place English walnut halves and red and green Maraschino cherries, cut in half, around the top of the cake. Dip walnut halves and cherries in a little honey to help them stick to the cake. To keep the cake moist, wrap it securely in plastic wrap while it is still warm.

Fruit Cake (cont'd)

Author's Note: I add a container of mixed candied fruit and candied cherries to this recipe. My Mom made several of these fruit cakes every year at Christmas. Many people avoid fruit cake, but this recipe makes an excellent cake. For years, I would never even try it, but once I did, I liked it so well that my Mom said I would take a slice of it to bed with me to eat while I was reading before going to sleep.

Wanda Huff Fruitcake
Priscilla Pyles Huff

2 cups sugar
2 sticks butter
4 eggs
½ cup buttermilk
2 cups flour
1 teaspoon salt
1 teaspoon soda
1 cup coconut
2 cups pecans, chopped
1 pound orange slice candy, cut up
8 ounces pitted dates, cut up
1-1/2 cups flour
1 cup frozen orange juice
2 cups powdered sugar

Stir orange slices and dates in 1-1/2 cups flour. Set aside.
Cream sugar, butter and eggs.
Add buttermilk, 2 cups of flour, salt and soda. Mix well.
Add coconut, pecans and orange slice mixture.
Pour into greased angel food tube pan.
Bake 2-1/2 hours at 250 degrees.

Mix orange juice and powdered sugar.
Pour over top of hot cake.
Cool and refrigerate overnight in pan.
Next day, remove from pan and store in airtight container in refrigerator to keep moist.

Cake is best if it sets 3 days before cutting.

Gingerbread Cake
Priscilla Pyles Huff

¾ cup bacon grease or lard
1 cup sugar
2 eggs
1 cup dark corn syrup or molasses
3 cups flour
2 teaspoons baking soda
1 teaspoon ginger
1 teaspoon cloves
1 teaspoon cinnamon
1 cup buttermilk

Cream bacon grease with sugar.
Add eggs, one at a time beating thoroughly after each egg.
Beat in corn syrup (or molasses).
Sift dry ingredients together.
Add dry ingredients alternately with buttermilk to wet mixture.
Beat smooth.
Pour in greased and floured 13"x9"x2" pan.

Bake at 350 degrees for 35-40 minutes.

Note: This recipe is about 150 years old. Very moist. I think it is best with corn syrup rather than molasses. Gives you a taste of time gone by, especially at Christmas.

Honey Bun Cake
Lori Means Underwood
Classic Stained Glass & Gift Gallery
250 Hoosier Street
North Vernon, IN 47265
812-346-4527

1 package yellow cake mix with pudding (18.25 ounce)
4 eggs
2/3 cup vegetable oil
1/3 cup water
8-ounce package sour cream
½ cup firmly packed brown sugar
1 teaspoon cinnamon
2/3 cup chopped pecans

Combine first five ingredients.
Beat at medium speed with mixer until smooth.
Set aside.

Combine brown sugar, cinnamon and pecans.
Set aside.

Grease and flour 9x13 pan.
Pour half of batter into pan.
Sprinkle with half of brown sugar mixture.

Pour balance of batter in pan.
Sprinkle with remaining brown sugar mixture.
Swirl batter with knife.

Bake at 350 degrees for 30-35 minutes or until toothpick comes out clean.

Honey Bun Cake (cont'd)

Glaze:

1 cup powdered sugar
2 tablespoons milk
½ teaspoon vanilla

Beat until smooth and drizzle glaze over warm cake.

Lemon-Coconut Pound Cake
Priscilla Pyles Huff

½ cup butter, softened
1-1/3 cups sugar
3 eggs
1-1/2 cups flour
½ teaspoon salt
1/8 teaspoon baking soda
½ cup sour cream
Zest of 1 lemon
1 cup coconut – divided

Beat softened butter.
Gradually add sugar and beat until light and fluffy.
Add eggs, one at a time and beat just until blended after each egg.
Sift together flour, salt and soda.
Add to butter mixture alternately with sour cream, beginning
and ending with flour mixture.
Beat on low speed until blended.
Stir in lemon zest and ½ cup coconut.
Pour batter into greased and floured 9"x5" loaf pan.
Bake at 325 degrees for 1 hour and 5 minutes.

Cool on wire rack 15 minutes.
Remove cake from pan to rack and cool completely about 1 hour.

Lemon Glaze:

2 cups powdered sugar
3 tablespoons milk
3 teaspoons lemon juice

Mix ingredients together and spoon over cake in fancy drizzles.
Sprinkle remaining coconut over glazed cake.

Love Light Chocolate Cake
Edna Tolliver Hayes Hollandsworth

2 eggs, separated
1-1/2 cups sugar
1-3/4 cups sifted cake flour (such as Softasilk)
¾ teaspoon baking soda
¾ teaspoon salt
1/3 cup Wesson oil
1 cup buttermilk
4 tablespoons Hershey's cocoa or,
    two 2-ounce squares of unsweetened chocolate, melted

Heat oven to 350 degrees.
Grease and flour two round layer 8" pans, 1-1/2" deep.
Beat egg whites until frothy.
Gradually beat in ½ cup of the sugar.
Continue beating until very stiff and glossy.
In another bowl, sift remaining sugar, flour, soda and salt.
Add Wesson oil and half of the buttermilk.
Beat 1 minute on medium speed mixer.
Scrape sides and bottom of bowl as you beat.
Add remaining buttermilk and egg yolks.
Beat 1 minute more, scraping bowl constantly.
Fold in meringue thoroughly by hand.
Pour into pans.
Jar pans on table top to break large bubbles.

Bake 30 to 35 minutes.
Frost with chocolate or fluffy icing.

Very good!

Lemonade Muffins
Mary Keller Kost

1-1/2 cups all-purpose flour
¼ cup white sugar
2-1/2 teaspoons baking powder
½ teaspoon salt
1 egg, beaten
1 6-ounce can (2/3 cup) frozen lemonade, thawed
¼ cup milk
1/3 cup cooking oil
½ cup walnuts, chopped

Mix dry ingredients.
Combine egg, ½ cup lemonade, milk and oil.
Add to dry ingredients and stir just until moistened.
Gently stir in nuts.
Fill greased muffin cups.
Bake at 375 degrees for 15-20 minutes or until done.
While hot, brush with remaining lemonade and sprinkle with white sugar.

Mexican Fruit Cake
Ellen Bryant Ritchie

1 20-ounce can crushed pineapple, undrained
2 cups flour
2 teaspoons soda
2 cups sugar
2 eggs
1 cup chopped nuts

Mix all ingredients and pour into greased 9x13 pan.
Bake at 350 degrees for 45 minutes.
Cover with frosting while warm.

Frosting:

1 8-ounce package cream cheese
2 cups powdered sugar
½ cup margarine, melted
1 teaspoon vanilla

Combine all ingredients and beat with mixer until smooth and creamy.
Frost Mexican Fruit Cake while warm.

Oatmeal Cake – Betty Lou Ritchie
Priscilla Pyles Huff

1-1/2 cups 1-minute quick oatmeal
1-1/2 sticks butter, softened
2-1/4 cups boiling water
1-1/2 cups light brown sugar
1-1/2 cups sugar
3 eggs
2-1/4 cups flour
¾ teaspoon salt
1-1/2 teaspoons baking soda
1-1/2 teaspoons cinnamon
1-1/2 teaspoons vanilla

Bring water to boiling in a saucepan with lid.
Add butter and stir in oats.
Remove from burner and cover with lid.
Let stand for 20 minutes.
Cream together brown sugar, sugar and eggs.
Add oatmeal, flour, salt, soda, cinnamon and vanilla.
Blend. Pour into ungreased 9"x13" baking pan.
Bake at 350 degrees for 35 to 45 minutes until toothpick comes out clean.

Topping:

1-1/2 cups brown sugar
1-1/2 sticks butter
¾ cup Milnot
1-1/2 cups coconut
1 cup pecans

Oatmeal Cake – Betty Lou Ritchie (cont'd)

Cook sugar, butter and Milnot in a saucepan or skillet on low-to-medium heat for about 5 minutes, stirring constantly.
Add coconut and pecans and stir.
Spread on cake.
Put under broiler for a few minutes, watching closely.

Oatmeal Cake
Burline Meddock (Mrs. Steve) Tolliver

1 cup quick oats
1-1/2 cup boiling water
1 cup brown sugar
1 cup white sugar
1 stick margarine
2 eggs, beaten
1 teaspoon vanilla
1 teaspoon baking soda
1 teaspoon cinnamon
½ teaspoon salt
1-1/2 cups flour

Pour hot water over oats and let stand 20 minutes.
Add margarine, white sugar and brown sugar.
Mix well.
Add eggs and vanilla.
Sift dry ingredients and add to above.
Bake in long flat pan 30 to 35 minutes at 350 degrees.

Topping

1 cup coconut
1 cup brown sugar
½ cup milk
4 tablespoons butter

Mix well and spread on warm cake.
Sit in broiler for just a few seconds.

Author's Note: Daughter Linda says they didn't have many sweets when they were young. This cake was moist and so good, and it really hit the spot when their mother made this Oatmeal Cake.

Pecan Pie Cake
Linda Tolliver Richard

1 package yellow cake mix
½ cup butter (1 stick), melted
4 eggs
1-1/2 cups light corn syrup
½ cup dark brown sugar, firmly packed
1 teaspoon vanilla
2 cups pecans, chopped

Heat oven to 325 degrees.
Place cake mix, melted butter and 1 egg in large mixer bowl.
Beat on low speed until well mixed, about 30 seconds.
Measure out 2/3 cup of batter and set aside.
Spread remaining batter in bottom of ungreased 9x13 baking dish.
Bake for 15 minute or until top lightly browns and puffs up.
Remove dish from oven and place on wire rack.
Cool for 10 minutes.
Leave oven on.

Place reserved 2/3 cup of batter, corn syrup, sugar, 3 eggs and vanilla in large mixer bowl.
Beat on low speed for one minute.
Stop mixer and scrape sides of bowl.
Beat on medium speed until well mixed, about 1 minute.
Fold in pecans.
Pour pecan mixture on top of warm cake in baking dish.
Gently smooth out evenly over cake.
Bake for 40 to 45 minutes or until edges are browned but middle is still soft.
Remove to wire rack and cool 30 minutes.
Serve plain or with vanilla ice cream.

This is delicious!!

Persimmon Cake
Vicki Agner Yates

1 cup persimmon pulp
½ cup sugar
1 egg
Butter – size of a walnut
1 cup flour
1 teaspoon baking powder
½ teaspoon soda

Combine persimmon pulp, sugar, egg, butter, flour, baking powder and soda.

Mix well and pour into a well-greased and floured pan.

Bake about 40 minutes in a moderate oven (about 350 degrees).

Pig Lickin' Cake
George James

1 box yellow cake mix
½ cup oil
4 eggs
1 can Mandarin oranges with juice (9 ounces)

Combine cake mix, oil, eggs and juice from oranges.
Add Mandarin oranges.
Pour into 2 round cake pans or a 9x13 pan.
Bake at 325 degrees for 30 minutes.
Cool.

Slice round cakes into 2 layers each.
If using a 9x13 dish, cut cake in half, then cut each half into 2 layers.

Topping:

18 ounces Cool Whip
1 can crushed pineapple, drained
1 large package vanilla instant pudding mix

Mix all ingredients.
Spread topping between layers of cake, stacking layers on top of each other.
You will end up with a 4-layer torte.
Save enough topping for the top.

Note: A torte is (1) a rich cake made with beaten eggs, nuts, fruit and little flour, or (2) a cake with thin layers of custard, sometimes preserved fruit and chocolate.

Mandarin Orange is a small, sweet, spicy citrus fruit with a thin orange-colored, very loose peel and segments that separate easily.

Pig Eating Cake
Carolyn Poling

1 yellow or orange cake mix
3 eggs
1 cup oil
1 large can Mandarin oranges, well drained

Mix all ingredients.
Bake at 350 degrees for 25 minutes in a 9" x 13" pan.
Cool!

Frosting

1 16-ounce can crushed pineapple with juice
1 medium container Cool Whip
1 package instant vanilla pudding

Mix all ingredients.
Frost the cool cake.

Keep in refrigerator.

Pumpkin Crunch Cake
Sara Turner Marbaugh

1 16-ounce can of pumpkin
1 12-ounce can evaporated milk
3 eggs
1-1/4 cups sugar
4 teaspoons pumpkin pie spice
½ teaspoon salt

1 package yellow cake mix
1 cup chopped pecans
1 cup melted butter

Preheat oven to 350 degrees.
Grease a 9x13 pan.

Combine the first 6 ingredients and pour into greased 9x13 pan.
Sprinkle on dry cake mix.
Sprinkle on chopped pecans.
Drizzle with butter.
Bake 50 minutes.
Serve with Cool Whip.

Enjoy!

Red Cake

Nell Chambers (Mrs. Roy) Tolliver

½ cup shortening
1-1/2 cups sugar
2 eggs
1 ounce red food coloring
2 tablespoons cocoa
1 teaspoon vanilla
1 teaspoon salt (scant)
1 cup buttermilk
1 teaspoon baking soda
2-1/2 cups cake flour
1 tablespoon vinegar

Cream shortening, sugar and eggs in mixer.

Make a paste of food coloring and cocoa.

Add to creamed mixture.

Add salt, flour, buttermilk and vanilla.

Remove from mixer and mix in vinegar and baking soda (*do not beat*).

Bake in two 8-inch layer pans at 350 degrees for 30 to 35 minutes. After cooling, cut the layers in half, making four layers.

Red Cake (cont'd)

Icing

3 tablespoons flour
1 cup water

Cook water and flour until thick. Cool.
1 cup sugar
1 cup butter
1 teaspoon vanilla

Cream these ingredients until fluffy. Add to the flour/water mixture and beat.

French Cream (use for topping or filling)

Nell Chambers (Mrs. Roy) Tolliver

2-1/2 pounds powdered sugar
½ pound oleo (butter or margarine)
1 pound shortening
½ cup water
Pinch of salt
½ teaspoon vanilla

Mix all ingredients on low speed for 20 minutes.

Author's Note: For a number of years, Aunt Nell cooked in the kitchen of the Lake White Club just south of Waverly, Ohio. She loved to bake, and her desserts were wonderfully delicious. However, as was the case with many older cooks, most of her recipes were kept in her head. Very few were written down. Her recipes shown in this publication were provided by her granddaughters.

Rum Cake
Granny Ackerman (submitted by Erica Wachter)

Cake:
1 cup chopped pecans or walnuts
1 18-1/2 ounce yellow cake mix
1 3-3/4 ounce Jell-O Vanilla Instant Pudding & Pie Filling
4 eggs
½ cup cold water
½ cup oil
½ cup Bacardi dark rum (80 proof)

Preheat oven to 325 degrees.
Grease and flour bundt pan.
Sprinkle nuts over bottom of pan.
Mix remaining cake ingredients together.
Pour batter over nuts.
Bake at 325 degrees for 1 hour.   Cool.
Invert on serving plate.
Prick top.

Glaze:
¼ pound butter
¼ cup water
1 cup sugar
½ cup rum

Melt butter in saucepan.
Stir in water and sugar.
Boil 5 minutes, stirring constantly.
Remove from heat.
Stir in rum.
Spoon and brush glaze evenly over top and sides of cake.

Sponge Cake - A Favorite!
Edna Tolliver Hayes Hollandsworth

2 eggs
¼ teaspoon salt
1 cup sugar
½ teaspoon lemon extract
½ teaspoon grated lemon rind, optional
½ cup milk
1 tablespoon butter
1 cup sifted flour (slightly more if using cake flour)
1 teaspoon baking powder

Beat eggs until very light.
Beat in salt, sugar, lemon extract and rind.
Heat milk and butter until boiling hot.
Beat in milk and butter.
Sift flour and baking powder together.
Beat in flour and baking powder mixture.
Pour very quickly into a well-greased and floured 8-inch square pan.

Bake immediately 25 to 30 minutes in 350-degree oven previously heated and ready.

Ice with white lemon icing or use Cool Whip topping.

Snow Ball Cake
Helen Salyer Perkins Johansen

1 cup hot water
1 package unflavored gelatin
1 cup sugar
1 cup pineapple juice
1 #2 can crushed pineapple
3 packages Dream Whip
1 angel food cake
1 3-1/2 ounce can flaked coconut
1 cup chopped pecans

Drain pineapple and save juice.
Dissolve gelatin in water in a saucepan.
Add sugar and pineapple juice.
Bring to a boil.
Add pineapple.
Refrigerate until partially thickened.
When partially thickened, fold in Dream Whip, saving some for topping.
In the bottom of a container with a lid, break up half of the angel food cake.
Layer with half of the refrigerated mixture.
Add another layer of broken up angel food cake.
Layer the balance of the refrigerated mixture.
Top with Dream Whip, coconut and pecans.
Store, covered, in refrigerator.

Author's Note: I don't know if Dream Whip is still readily available, but Cool Whip works great!!

Grandma's Stack Cake / Cookies
Willa Tolliver Salyer Lyons

1 egg
¾ cup sugar
½ cup Crisco
½ cup sorghum (molasses)
½ cup buttermilk
2 teaspoons baking soda
2 teaspoons ginger
½ teaspoon salt
5-6 cups all-purpose flour

Mix egg, sugar, Crisco, sorghum, buttermilk, soda, ginger and salt. Mix well.
Stir in three (3) cups of flour.
Add additional flour until dough is stiff.
Turn out onto floured counter or bread board and knead (adding flour as necessary) until dough can be shaped into a flat ball (about 2 cups of flour).
Cut dough into six (6) equal parts.
Roll each piece to size of the bottom of a cake pan.
If piece is too large or too small, it can be pushed with your fingers to fit cake pan.
Bake at 350 degrees about 20 minutes or until light brown.

As cakes are finished, put apple butter or cooked dried apples between each layer while cakes are hot. Do not put apple butter or dried apples on top of cake.
If you have two cake pans, layers can be baked two at a time.

Cake keeps for several days but should be refrigerated after the first day as the apples will mold easily.
Cake can also be frozen, and pieces cut as needed without thawing.

Grandma's Stack Cake / Cookies (cont'd)

Cake is best served by cutting it in half, then slicing sideways rather than pie-shaped pieces.

Dough can be rolled out thin and cut with cookie cutter or rolled into walnut-sized balls and flattened to make **"Sweet Biscuits."**

Place on cookie sheet and bake at 350 degrees for 12 to 14 minutes.

Author's Note: Grandma's Stack Cake is a plain cake but took a lot of strength to mix by hand since it is a very stiff dough. Mom always made this cake for the family reunion. It was one of Uncle Steve's favorite cakes and Mom would cut out a large section of the cake and put it in a separate container just for him. As a child, my Mom said that Grandma kept a bag of these cookies on the steps leading to the upstairs and the children could get one of these cookies out of that sack any time they wanted one!

Texas Cake
Ruby Brady (Mrs. Leck) Tolliver

2 cups flour
2 eggs
½ teaspoon salt
2 cups sugar
2 tablespoons pineapple, crushed and drained

Mix all cake ingredients.
Pour into a 10 inch x 15 inch jelly roll pan (1 inch deep)
Bake at 325 degrees for 35 minutes.

Icing

1 can German chocolate cake icing
1 cup sugar
1 stick butter, melted
1 cup milk

Mix all ingredients in saucepan.
Bring to a boil and boil 1 minute.

Pour icing over cake as soon as it comes from the oven.

ENJOY!

Author's Note: Daughter Wanda doesn't remember her Mom baking a lot and that was why this Texas Sheet Cake was always special. It wasn't something they had on a regular basis. This is about the only recipe her Mommy had written down, but it surely was a great one!

Texas Sheet Cake
Mark Kaufman

Mix in bowl:
- 2 cups flour
- 2 cups sugar
- (set aside)

Put in pan and bring to a boil:
- 2 sticks margarine
- 3 tablespoons cocoa
- 1 cup water

Pour this mixture over flour and sugar mixture.

Add:
- ½ cup buttermilk
- 2 eggs
- 1 teaspoon vanilla
- 1 teaspoon baking soda
- ½ teaspoon salt

Pour into greased and floured sheet cake pan. Bake at 400 degrees for 20 minutes.

Icing

Place in saucepan:

- 1 stick margarine
- 3 tablespoons cocoa
- 1/3 cup buttermilk

Boil till slightly thickened.

Texas Sheet Cake (cont'd)

Remove and add:

>1 lb. powdered sugar
>1 teaspoon vanilla
>1 cup nuts, optional

Spread on hot cake.

Note: Mark says that he starts making the icing immediately after putting the cake in the oven, using the same pan as he used for the cake. No need to wash it!

Vanilla Blueberry Loaf Cake
Mindy Toppin Gallagher

1-1/2 cups all-purpose flour, plus 2 tablespoons
1-1/2 cups fresh or frozen blueberries (thawed and drained, if using frozen)
1 cup sugar
1 cup (2 sticks) unsalted butter, softened
½ cup Greek yogurt
3 eggs
1-1/2 teaspoons vanilla extract
1 teaspoon lemon zest
1 teaspoon baking powder
¾ teaspoon salt
Powdered sugar, garnish

Preheat oven to 350 degrees.
Grease a 9x5-inch loaf pan with butter or non-stick spray.
Mix 1-1/2 cups flour, baking powder and salt together in a mixing bowl and set aside.
In a large bowl or mixer, cream together butter and sugar until fluffy and lightened in color. 4-5 minutes.
One at a time, beat in eggs, waiting for each to be incorporated before adding the next.
Mix in vanilla extract and lemon zest.
In batches, alternate between adding in flour mixture and Greek yogurt, beginning and ending with the dry ingredients.
Mix until only just combined.
In a separate bowl, toss blueberries in remaining flour (this prevents them from sinking to the bottom of your loaf pan), then gently fold them into your batter.
Pour batter into greased loaf pan and place in oven.

Vanilla Blueberry Loaf Cake (cont'd)

Bake 55 minutes, or until toothpick inserted in center comes out clean.
Remove from oven and let cool 20-30 minutes before removing from pan.
Dust generously with powdered sugar and serve warm or at room temperature.

White Walnut Cake
Knox County, Kentucky

½ cup butter
1 cup sugar
½ cup milk
1-1/2 cup cake flour
3 egg whites, stiffly beaten
¾ cup walnuts, chopped and floured
1 teaspoon cream of tartar
½ teaspoon baking soda, dissolved in 1 teaspoon milk

Preheat oven to 350 degrees.
Cream butter and sugar.
Add milk and flour, alternately.
Add eggs and nuts and beat until smooth.
Add cream of tartar and the dissolved baking soda.
Beat well.
Bake in two 8-inch layer pans, well-greased for 20-25 minutes.

Seven Minute White Frosting

2 egg whites, unbeaten
1-1/2 cups sugar
5 tablespoons cold water
¼ teaspoon cream of tartar *
1 teaspoon vanilla

Place egg whites, sugar, cold water and cream of tartar in top of double boiler over rapidly boiling water.
Beat constantly with electric mixer for 7 minutes.
Remove frosting from heat.
Add vanilla. Continue beating until frosting is the right consistency to be spread.
* 1-1/2 teaspoon of light corn syrup can be substituted for the cream of tartar.

Zucchini Cake
Carolyn Poling

3 cups grated zucchini
3 cups sugar
1 cup corn oil
4 eggs
3 cups flour
1 teaspoon soda
½ teaspoon salt
1-1/2 teaspoons cinnamon
2 teaspoons baking powder
1 cup chopped walnuts
1 teaspoon vanilla
1 banana, smashed

Preheat oven to 350 degrees.
Cream first 4 ingredients.
Then combine dry ones.
Add walnuts, vanilla and banana.
Mix well and pour into two 4-inch bread pans – greased and floured.
Bake for 1 hour and 15 minutes.

Frosting:

3 ounces cream cheese
¼ cup soft butter
2 cups powdered sugar
1 teaspoon vanilla

Mix well and spread on cake.

Notes:

CANDIES

Buckeyes
Opal Tolliver Bowles Ruble

1-1/2 sticks butter
1-1/2 cups peanut butter
1 tablespoon vanilla
1 pound box powdered sugar (3-3/4 cups)
1 package chocolate chips (12 ounces)
½ bar paraffin

Combine butter, peanut butter, vanilla and powdered sugar.

Mix well.

Make into small balls and place on cookie sheet or waxed paper.

Chill for several hours or overnight.

Melt chocolate chips and paraffin in double boiler.

Using a toothpick, dunk balls into melted chocolate mixture, leaving a dime-sized part of the ball without chocolate so the finished ball looks like a buckeye.

Makes 5 to 6 dozen.

Note: Dipping chocolate can be used instead of the chocolate chips and paraffin.

Author's Note: Interesting information:

What is a Buckeye?

- ✓ An inedible nut which resembles the eye of a deer—Buck-eye!
- ✓ Ohio's state tree.
- ✓ An Ohio resident.
- ✓ A legendary protector against arthritis when carried in one's pocket.
- ✓ A traditional piece of candy made to resemble the nut.

Pulled Cream Candy
(Vinegar Candy)
Willa Tolliver Salyer Lyons

1 cup sugar
1-1/2 teaspoon baking powder
1 tablespoon vinegar
¼ stick butter
3 tablespoons boiling water
Pinch of salt

Mix all ingredients in saucepan.
Bring to a boil and cook to hard boil stage on candy thermometer (2 marks above 250 degrees).
Pour onto cabinet or marble slab. If you want to make different colors, pour in several puddles.
Let cool until you can handle it.
Add vanilla.
Add food coloring (if desired).

Pull sections as much as you possibly can. Like pulling taffy.
Pull into long twisted ropes and cut into "pillows" with scissors.
Put pieces between waxed paper to allow them to cream.

Author's Note: Mom got this recipe from Zona Young in Ashland, Kentucky. She was the sister of Mom's second husband, Everett Lyons. As is the case with the Stack Cake, this recipe requires quite a bit of physical strength unless you happen to have a "puller" like one used in a taffy shop. But when the candy creams and you plop one of the little pillows in your mouth, the taste and texture are wonderful.

Easy Fantasy Fudge, Option #1
Willa Tolliver Salyer Lyons

¾ cup butter (1-1/2 sticks)
3 cups sugar
2/3 cup evaporated milk
1 package chocolate chips
1 jar marshmallow crème
1 cup nuts, optional
1 teaspoon vanilla

Grease pan or plate with additional margarine.
Combine margarine, sugar and milk in a heavy pan.
Bring to a full rolling boil on medium heat.
Continue boiling 5 minutes or until candy thermometer reaches 234 degrees, stirring constantly.
Remove from heat.
Add chips and stir until melted.
Add marshmallow crème, nuts and vanilla.
Pour into pan or plate, cool and cut!

Easy Fantasy Fudge, Option #2

¾ cup butter (1-1/2 sticks)
3 cups sugar
2/3 cup evaporated milk
1 jar marshmallow crème
1 teaspoon vanilla
3 tablespoons Creamy Jif Peanut Butter

Grease pan or plate with additional margarine.
Combine margarine, sugar and milk in a heavy pan.
Bring to a full rolling boil on medium heat.
Continue boiling 5 minutes or until candy thermometer reaches 234 degrees, stirring constantly.
Remove from heat.
Add marshmallow crème, vanilla and peanut butter.

Beat until the fudge thickens and loses its shine.
Pour onto plate, cool and cut.

Peanut Butter Fudge
Bea Ruggles

3 cups sugar
¾ cup margarine
2/3 cup evaporated milk
1 cup peanut butter (any kind)
2-1/2 cups miniature marshmallows
1 teaspoon vanilla

Combine sugar, margarine and milk in a heavy saucepan.
Bring to a full boil, stirring constantly.
Continue to boil for 5 minutes.
Remove from heat.
Add peanut butter, marshmallows and vanilla.
Mix with a hand mixer.
When mixed well, pour into a 9x13 buttered dish.
Cool.

Makes 3 pounds

Green Cookbook Peanut Butter Fudge
Helen Salyer Perkins Johansen

2 cups sugar
3 tablespoons white Karo syrup
Pinch of salt
¾ cup milk
3 tablespoons peanut butter
1 tablespoon butter
½ teaspoon vanilla

Combine sugar, syrup, salt and milk in a heavy saucepan.
Bring to a full boil on medium heat.
Lower heat so the mixture continues a slow boil but doesn't run over.
Continue cooking mixture until it turns to a light tan color and forms a soft ball when a few drops are placed in cold water.
If using a candy thermometer, bring to soft boil stage.
Remove from heat.
Add peanut butter, butter and vanilla.
Mix well, then continue beating until it begins to thicken, and the surface looks dull. You can set the pan in the sink in an inch or so of cold water to aid in cooling as you beat.
Pour onto a buttered plate or platter.
As the fudge begins to set, score where you want to cut.
When cool, continue to cut on score marks.

Note: To make Chocolate Fudge, add 2 tablespoons of cocoa with the sugar, syrup, salt and milk and eliminate the peanut butter.

Pumpkin Fudge
Opal Tolliver Bowles Ruble

3 cups sugar
½ teaspoon cornstarch
1/8 teaspoon salt
Sprinkle of cinnamon, nutmeg, allspice and cloves.
½ cup Carnation evaporated milk
6 teaspoons cooked and sieved pumpkin
2/3 package miniature marshmallows
1 teaspoon vanilla
Chopped nuts, if desired

Mix all dry ingredients in a heavy saucepan.
Add milk and pumpkin.
Cook to the soft ball stage.
Remove from heat.
Add vanilla and marshmallows.
Stir until marshmallows are melted.
Set aside to cool until barely warm.
Beat until creamy and thick.
Pour into buttered dish and let cool.
Cut into squares before completely cold.
Add nut meats before beating, if desired.

Family Notes
From Edna Tolliver Hayes Hollandsworth's daughter, Audrey Hayes Wilson

My Mother started weeks before Christmas making fudge and sold it for Christmas presents. She gave all the money she made to Christian missions. I don't know if Mother's baked chicken was in the recipes, I gave you. (Yes, it was and is included in this book.) That one was one of my favorite meals along with homemade bread and green beans she had grown in her garden and canned, so we had plenty all year around. Also, I loved her glorified rice.

We had apple trees and she would make apple pie filling and put it in jars. She could make a meal and could make apple pie any time anyone would come by. It was rare that we didn't have someone eating with us or staying with us. I did not inherit my Mom's talent for cooking, but I did inherit the habit of having company and having people live with us. I did learn to put meals on the table quickly (but not as good as Mothers). I think my girls inherited my Mom's cooking talent.

Buttery Peanut Brittle
Jim Purnell

2 cups granulated sugar
1 cup light corn syrup
½ cup water
1 cup butter or margarine
2 cups raw or roasted peanuts
1 teaspoon soda

Combine sugar, corn syrup and water in a heavy 3-quart saucepan.
Cook and stir until sugar dissolves.
When syrup boils, blend in butter.
Stir frequently after mixture reaches the syrup stage (230 degrees) on a candy thermometer.
Add nuts when the temperature reaches soft-crack stage (280 degrees).
Stir constantly until temperature reaches the hard-crack stage (305 degrees).
Remove from heat.
Quickly stir in soda, mixing thoroughly.
Pour onto two buttered cookie sheets or onto a buttered marble slab.

As the candy cools, stretch it out thin by lifting and pulling from edges, using two forks.
Loosen from pans or slab as soon as possible and turn candy over.
Break into pieces.

Makes 2-1/2 pounds.

Notes:

CASSEROLES

Blueberry Buckle
Lori Tolliver Holberg

1 stick butter, softened
¾ cup sugar
1 teaspoon vanilla
¼ teaspoon baking powder
1-1/3 cups flour
½ teaspoon salt
3 large eggs
3 cups blueberries

Using an electric mixer, in a medium bowl, cream together butter and sugar, then beat in vanilla.
In a small bowl, stir together baking powder, flour and salt.
Beat flour mixture into butter mixture alternating with the eggs, one at a time.
Beat well after each addition.
Fold in blueberries.
Spread the batter in a well-buttered 2-quart baking dish.

Topping:

1 stick cold butter, cut into bits
1 cup sugar
2/3 cup flour
1 teaspoon cinnamon
1 teaspoon nutmeg

Combine all ingredients and sprinkle evenly over the batter.

Bake at 350 degrees for 45-50 minutes.

Note: Blueberry Buckle is always a must in July after picking our own fresh blueberries!

Bread Dressing/Stuffing
Helen Salyer Perkins Johansen

2 loaves bread (2-4 day old bread is best)
½ cup butter or margarine
¾ cup chopped onion
1-1/2 cups chopped celery, stalks and leaves
2 eggs, lightly beaten
1 teaspoon salt
1 teaspoon pepper
1 tablespoon dried sage
Turkey or chicken broth

Break bread into small pieces and allow to dry overnight either on the counter or in a large bowl covered with a tea towel or paper towels.
Melt butter or margarine in a skillet.
Add onions and celery, cover and cook slowly until celery is tender, stirring occasionally.
Add salt, pepper and sage to dried bread and stir lightly.
Add onion/celery mixture and lightly beaten eggs.
Add turkey or chicken broth as needed; probably 1-2 cups. If you don't have enough broth, hot water can be added.
Bread should be thoroughly moistened, but not soupy.
Pour mixture into a 9x13 baking dish that has been sprayed with cooking spray (Pam, etc.)

Bake in 350-degree oven about 30-45 minutes or until top is golden brown.

If desired, 1 cup of oysters can be added prior to adding the broth. Dressing can be divided into 2 smaller baking dishes and oysters added to just one of the dishes.

Bread Dressing/Stuffing (cont'd)

Corn bread can be used instead of part or all of the bread.
Turkey can be stuffed with dressing but should not be stuffed until just before roasting. *See Roasting a Turkey under the Meat section.* Remove stuffing from bird immediately after the meal and place in a separate container for storing.

Breakfast Casserole
Lori Tolliver Holberg

1 lb. hot sausage
24-ounce bag frozen hash browns, thawed
3 cups shredded cheddar cheese
½ teaspoon salt
¼ cup green pepper, chopped
¼ cup red pepper, chopped
12 eggs, beaten
2 cups milk

Lightly grease a 9x13 pan.
Spread hash browns on bottom of pan.
Sprinkle salt over hash browns.
Brown sausage, crumble and drain
Layer sausage, cheese and peppers over hash browns.
Combine milk and beaten eggs and pour over mixture.

Bake at 350 degrees for 50 minutes.

Note: This recipe can be prepared a day ahead; just wait until you're ready to put it in the over before adding the milk and egg mixture. The casserole became known as "Company Casserole" at our house since I always served it when we had overnight friends or family visiting.

Broccoli Casserole
Gladys Hamilton Green

2 or 3 stalks fresh broccoli or 2 packages frozen broccoli
2 eggs, beaten
½ cup Miracle Whip
1 cup cheddar cheese, shredded
1 can cream of mushroom or cream of celery soup
Salt and pepper, to taste

Cup up broccoli and boil 5 minutes.
If using frozen broccoli, thaw it out but do not cook.
Combine all ingredients in mixing bowl.
Pour into buttered 6x10 oblong or 9-nch round casserole dish.
Top with crumbled snack crackers – Ritz or HiHo

Bake at 350 degrees for 35 minutes.

Cabbage Au Gratin
Opal Tolliver Bowles Ruble

1 medium head cabbage
1 small onion
Velveeta cheese slices
Crushed crackers
Milk
Buttered bread crumbs

Trim and wash cabbage.
Cut into small pieces.
Put in saucepan with small amount of water and steam until wilted – do not overcook.
Drain.
Put half of the cabbage in a casserole dish.
Cut up one half of the onion onto the cabbage, then crumble crackers on onion to cover well.
Layer with cheese slices.
Add remainder of cabbage, onion and crackers.
Add more cheese slices.
Pour enough milk over mixture to see it around the edges.
Top with buttered bread or cracker crumbs.
You can add red and green sweet peppers to the cabbage, if desired.

Bake at 350 degrees until bubbly and golden brown.

Cabbage, Sausage & Potato Casserole
Hans Johansen, Jr.

4 cup potatoes, cubed
2 tablespoons parsley, freeze dried
1 head cabbage, cut into chunks
1 pound sausage, browned and drained
3 cans chicken broth

Layer ingredients in a 9x13 ungreased pan with potatoes on the bottom and sausage on top.
Pour chicken broth or 3 cups hot water mixed with 6 chicken bouillon cubes over ingredients.
Cover with foil and place on a cookie sheet to prevent run over.

Bake at 375 degrees for 2 hours.

Check after 1 hour and push ingredients down into broth.

Check after 2 hours; may need more cooking time.

Liquid will absorb a little once it comes out of the oven.

Easy Chicken Casserole
Karen Tolliver Kratzer

2 cups cooked chicken, shredded
1 cup celery, chopped
1 cup mayonnaise
1 can cream of chicken soup
Sliced almonds, if desired
Shredded cheddar cheese
Potato chips, crumbled

Put first 5 ingredients in casserole dish.

Sprinkle crumbled potato chips on top.

Cover and bake at 350 degrees for 45 minutes.
Remove from oven and sprinkle shredded cheddar cheese on top.
Bake til cheese is melted.

Chicken Casserole Supreme
Hans Johansen, Jr.

3 cups cooked chunk chicken
2 cups celery, finely chopped
2-3 tablespoons minced onion
¾ cup Hellman's mayonnaise
1 cup cooked rice
1 can water chestnuts, drained and sliced
1 can cream of chicken soup

Combine all ingredients.

Spread into 9x13 baking dish.

Topping:

1 stick margarine
1 cup crushed corn flakes
½ cup sliced almonds

Combine all ingredients and cook in saucepan on top of stove until browned.

Crumble topping evenly over chicken.

Bake uncovered for 45 minutes at 350 degrees.

Hint: Make topping mixture first so it can have time to cool.

Corn Bread Pie
Baltimore and Ohio Railroad
Dinner in the Diner Cookbook

1 lb. ground beef
1 large onion, chopped
1 can tomato soup
2 cups water
1 teaspoon salt
¾ teaspoon pepper
1 tablespoon chili powder
½ cup green peppers
1 cup whole kernel corn

Brown the ground beef and onion in a skillet.
Add soup, water, seasonings, corn and green pepper.
Mix well and allow to simmer for 15 minutes.
Then fill a greased pie dish or casserole ¾ full, leaving room for the corn bread topping.

To make corn bread top, sift together the following:

¾ cup corn meal
1 tablespoon sugar
1 tablespoon flour
½ teaspoon salt
1-1/2 teaspoon baking powder

Corn Bread Pie (cont'd)

After they are sifted together, add:

1 egg, beaten
½ cup milk
1 tablespoon butter, melted

Stir lightly and fold in melted butter.
Cover the meat mixture with this topping and bake in a medium oven at 350 degrees for 18 to 20 minutes.

Don't be surprised when the topping disappears in the meat mixture.
It will rise during the baking and form a good layer of corn bread!

Don't be surprised when the whole dish disappears after you put it on the table, because it has been one of the most popular dishes - with both men and women – served on the Baltimore and Ohio!

Corn Pudding
Sharon Ross Beck

1 can (16 ounce) corn, cream-style
1 can (16 ounce) corn, whole kernel
8 ounces sour cream
½ stick margarine, melted
1 box Jiffy Corn Muffin Mix

Mix all ingredients together.

Pour into an 8x12 baking dish that has been coated inside with vegetable oil or sprayed with Pam.

Bake at 400 degrees for 25-30 minutes.

Note: The pudding will not be very brown.

Patricia's Dressing
Alice Ogez Litzy Perkins

½ loaf of fresh bread
Turkey or chicken drippings
1 heaping tablespoon sage
Salt and pepper to taste

Break fresh bread (do not dry) up in small pieces in mixing bowl.
Add drippings until bread is completely soaked and mixture is gooey.
Add sage.
Salt and pepper to taste.
You can taste the mixture since all ingredients are precooked.
Place in glass baking dish.

Bake at 325 degrees approximately 30 minutes until browned.

Dressing will still be gooey on the inside but will set as it cools.

Note: When Alice and her siblings were young, they would not eat dressing with onions or celery in it. Her mother, Patricia, came up with this recipe and it is the only dressing Alice will eat to this day.

Green Bean Bake
Helen Salyer Perkins Johansen

1 can cream of mushroom soup (10-3/4 ounces)
½ cup milk
1 teaspoon soy sauce
1 dash pepper
4 cups cooked cut green beans, drained
1 can French Fried Onions (2.8 ounces)

Mix soup, milk, soy sauce, pepper, beans and ½ can onions in a 1-1/2-quart casserole.

Bake at 350 degrees for 25 minutes or until hot.

Stir and sprinkle with remaining onions.

Bake 5 minutes more.

Serves 6

Hash Brown Breakfast Casserole
Victoria House Bed & Breakfast
Dana Graham Perkins

3 tablespoons oil
1 medium onion, chopped
2 lbs. shredded hash browns
1 lb. sausage
10 whole eggs, beaten
2 cups shredded cheddar cheese
Salt and pepper

Fry hash browns in the oil according to package directions until the potatoes begin to brown.
Spray a 9x13 baking dish with cooking spray.
Layer the hash browns in the bottom of the baking dish.
Top with cooked sausage.
Pour beaten eggs over hash browns and sausage.
Season eggs to taste.
Gently stir to coat hash browns and sausage with eggs.
Sprinkle cheese on top.

Refrigerate overnight.

Bake at 375 degrees for 40-50 minutes.

O'Brien Potato Casserole
Hans Johansen, Jr.

1 bag O'Brien frozen potatoes
2 cans cream of chicken soup
2 cups shredded cheddar cheese
½ pint sour cream
1 dash Morton's Nature Seasons Seasoning Blend
Town House Crackers

Combine all ingredients except crackers.
Pour into 3-quart casserole.

Bake covered at 375 degrees for 1 hour.

Top with crumbled crackers and bake 5-10 minutes longer.

Rice Casserole
Dorcas Neidig

1 stick butter
1 can Campbells beef consume or beef broth
1 can Campbells French onion soup
1 cup uncooked rice
1-2 small cans of sliced mushrooms

Melt butter in a 9x13 pan in oven while it is preheating to 400 degrees.
Add soups, rice and mushrooms.
Bake alone or add browned pork chops, pork tenderloin slices or chicken on top.

Bake for approximately 45 minutes.

Note: This recipe came out of the cookbook of Mrs. Neidig's Dad. He would handwrite his favorite recipes and tape them in his cookbook. He used Betty Crocker's Good and Easy Cook Book. This cookbook still gets much use today.

Susan's Shrimp Casserole
Joan Neuenschwander Schug

1 can mushroom soup
2 tablespoons chopped green bell pepper
2 tablespoons chopped onion
2 tablespoons melted butter
1 tablespoon lemon juice
½ teaspoon dry mustard
1 teaspoon Worcestershire sauce
¼ teaspoon pepper
1 cup cooked wild rice (Uncle Ben's Original Recipe)
1 cup cooked white rice
1 cup sharp cheddar cheese, cubed
½ pound salad shrimp, thawed

Combine first 8 ingredients.
Add rice, cheese and shrimp.
Pour into lightly buttered casserole dish.

Bake at 350 degrees for 30-35 minutes until bubbly.

Sweet Potato Casserole #1
Susan Matthews Wisecup

3 cups cooked sweet potatoes, mashed
1 cup sugar (could use a little less because topping is so sweet)
2 eggs, beaten
½ cup milk
½ teaspoon salt
6 tablespoons melted butter
1 teaspoon vanilla

Mix all ingredients together and put in greased casserole dish. (I use an 11" x 7" glass pan)

Topping:

1 cup brown sugar
½ cup flour
1 cup pecans, chopped
¼ cup butter, melted

Combine all ingredients.
Crumble over top of sweet potato mixture.

Bake uncovered at 350 degrees for 35-40 minutes.

Note: Taken from the "Freedom Tour" recipe book.

Sweet Potato Casserole #2
Fran Bruce – Grandmother of Pastor Jon Beck

3 cups cooked sweet potatoes
1 cup sugar
1 teaspoon vanilla
½ cup butter

Mix thoroughly in electric mixer.
Pour into buttered 9x13 casserole dish.
Spread top with Pecan Topping.

Pecan Topping:

1 cup light brown sugar
1/3 cup flour
1 cup chopped pecans
1/3 cup butter

Mix all ingredients with a fork.
Layer on top of sweet potato mixture.

Bake at 350 degrees for 30 minutes.

Toad in the Hole
Jim Iverson

1-1/2 to 2-1/2 lbs. <u>very coarsely ground</u> round steak
2-3 cups <u>thin</u> Bisquick Pancake Mix or other pancake mix (prepared as for pancakes)
2 tablespoons butter or margarine
Salt and pepper, to taste

Butter a 2-3 quart casserole.
Drop in ground round <u>very loosely</u> to a 3/4 – 1 inch layer.
Pour thin pancake mix over ground round layer.
Repeat layering and pouring until casserole dish is to within an inch or so from the top (pancake batter will rise slightly.)
Place butter or margarine pats on top, if desired.
Salt and pepper layers as you go.
Bake in 250-275 degree oven for approximately 2 hours or until top is browned.
The pieces of ground round will "peek" out of the baked batter, thus giving it the name "Toad in the Hole"!
Serve hot or cold – with catsup!

The key to this dish is to allow the coarsely ground round to have plenty of air surrounding the meat particles, thereby permitting the thin batter to intermingle throughout the dish. Regular ground hamburger just will not work!

This is a very simple recipe which can be adjusted in volume to serve few or many people.

This recipe was obtained from an Iowa weekly newspaper in the later 30's or early 40's. The identical recipe with the same name was in a Sunday supplement of a newspaper in the early 70's as movie actor Vincent Price's favorite!

Triple-Cheese Macaroni
Bob Keller

1 package (16 ounces) elbow macaroni
2 eggs
1 can (12 ounces) evaporated milk
¼ cup butter, melted
2 tablespoons prepared mustard
1 teaspoon seasoned salt
1 teaspoon pepper
8 ounces process cheese (Velveeta), melted
2 cups shredded mild cheddar cheese, *divided*
2 cups shredded sharp cheddar cheese, *divided*

Cook macaroni according to package directions.
Meanwhile, in a large bowl, whisk the eggs, milk, butter, mustard, seasoned salt and pepper until combined.
Stir in the process cheese and 1-1/2 cups of each cheddar cheese.
Drain macaroni and stir into cheese mixture.
Pour into a greased 3-quart baking dish.
Top with remaining cheeses.

Bake uncovered at 350 degrees for 25-30 minutes or until cheese is melted and edges are bubbly.

Yield: 6 servings

Vegetable Medley Casserole
Priscilla Pyle Huff

1 16-ounce bag frozen vegetables: broccoli, cauliflower, carrots, thawed and drained
1 can cream of mushroom soup
1 cup shredded Swiss cheese
1/3 cup sour cream
¼ teaspoon pepper
1 jar pimentos, chopped
1 can French onion rings

Mix all ingredients except onion rings.

Pour in sprayed casserole dish.

Top with onion rings.

Bake at 350 degrees for 30 minutes.

CHEESECAKES

Cherry Cheesecake Lush

Mary Etta Roth
Grateful Grubb Family Restaurant
412 South Madison Avenue
North Vernon, IN 47265
812-346-0004

1 cup vanilla wafer crumbs
1 cup finely chopped pecans
1 stick butter, softened

1 8-ounce package cream cheese, softened
1 cup powdered sugar
1 16-ounce container Cool Whip, divided
2 small boxes instant cheesecake pudding mix
3 cups milk
1 can cherry pie filling
½ cup chopped pecans

In a medium bowl, combine vanilla wafer crumbs, 2 cups finely chopped pecans and butter.
Press into 9x13 baking dish.
Bake 15 minutes at 350 degrees.
Remove from oven and let cool completely.

In separate bowl, combine cream cheese, powdered sugar and 1-1/2 cups of Cool Whip.
Mix until smooth.
Spread evenly over cooled crust.
Combine pudding mix, milk and 1 cup Cool Whip until smooth.
Spread evenly over cream cheese layer.
Top with cherry pie filling, Cool Whip and ½ cup chopped pecans.

Triple Chocolate Cheesecake
Jessica Ward

Crust:

1-1/4 cup chocolate graham crackers, crushed
2 tablespoons sugar
1/3 cup butter, melted

Mix together and press into pie plate or spring form pan.

Filling:

3 8-ounce packages cream cheese, softened
2/3 cups sugar
3 8-ounce packages semi-sweet Baker's chocolate squares
½ cup heavy cream
2 teaspoons vanilla
3 eggs

Melt and cool 2 packages of the chocolate squares.
Mix all ingredients except the chocolate until smooth.
Add chocolate and mix well.

Preheat oven to 325 degrees.
Pour filling into crust and bake for 45-50 minutes.
Let stand one hour to cool.
Melt the remaining chocolate package of chocolate squares and drizzle over top of cheesecake.

Chill and serve.

Miracle Cheese Cake
Dorcas Neidig

2 tablespoons powdered sugar
2 packages honey graham crackers, crushed
½ cup butter or margarine, softened
1 3-ounce package lemon gelatin
1 cup boiling water
1 13-ounce can Milnot, chilled
1 tablespoon vanilla
1 8-ounce package cream cheese
1 cup sugar

Roll graham crackers until fine.
Add sugar and margarine.
Pat into 13x9 pan, reserving ½ cup for the topping.
Press firmly as this forms a crust.

In a small, deep bowl, mix lemon gelatin with boiling water.
Let set to consistency of jelly.
Beat Milnot and vanilla on high speed of mixer until high peaks form. Chilling bowl and Milnot speeds beating time.
Keep cold.
In small mixing bowl, beat cream cheese and sugar on medium speed until smooth.
Add gelatin mixture slowly to keep smooth.
Fold into Milnot mixture.
Pour into crust and sprinkle top with ½ cup reserved crumbs.

Let set 10-12 hours in the refrigerator.

COOKIES

Alice Cookies
Mary Richardson

½ cup Crisco
¾ cup sugar
1 cup raisin
1 cup nuts
1 teaspoon baking powder
2 eggs
¼ cup milk
½ cup coconut
1 cup flour
½ teaspoon salt
1 cup oatmeal
1 teaspoon cinnamon

Blend Crisco and sugar.
Add eggs and milk.
Add coconut, raisins and nuts.
Sift baking powder, cinnamon and flour.
Add oatmeal to flour mixture.
Add this mixture to the Crisco, sugar, egg, milk, coconut, raisin and nut mixture.
Stir thoroughly.
Drop from spoon onto Crisco greased cookie sheets.

Bake in moderate over – 350 degrees – for 12 minutes.

Chinese Chews
Sheila Poole-Richart

½ cup butter
½ cup brown sugar
1 cup flour

1 cup brown sugar
2 eggs
1 teaspoon vanilla
½ teaspoon salt
½ teaspoon baking powder
1 cup coconut
1 cup pecans
Powdered sugar

Mix ½ cup butter, ½ cup brown sugar and flour.
Spread evenly in a 9x13 baking pan.
Press down.
Bake 10 minutes in a 350-degree oven.

Mix 1 cup brown sugar, eggs, vanilla, salt, baking powder, coconut and pecans.
Spread over baked "crust" and bake for 20 minutes in a 350-degree oven.
Cut into squares.
While still warm, roll in powdered sugar.

Chocolate Chip Cookies
Dorothy Atkinson Ristoff

1 cup Crisco
½ cup white sugar
1 cup brown sugar
2 eggs
1 teaspoon vanilla

Mix together with a wooden spoon.
Mixture will be lumpy.

DO NOT USE A MIXER!

2 cups plus 4 tablespoons flour
1 teaspoon baking soda
1 teaspoon salt

Mix together.

1 regular size bag semi-sweet chocolate chips

Add flour mixture and chips to Crisco/sugar mixture.
Stir with a spoon just for a little bit.
Put a baggie on your hands and mix with your hands.
Pick up a medium size bit of dough and shape but don't roll into a ball.
Place on cookie sheet.
Bake at 375 degrees for 10-12 minutes – maybe longer according to your oven.

This is a double batch. Makes about 30-34 cookies – more or less.

Coconut Macaroons
Mary Richardson

2-1/4 cups flour
1/3 teaspoon baking soda
2 teaspoons baking powder
½ teaspoon salt
1-1/4 cups shortening
1 cup granulated sugar
1 cup brown sugar
2 eggs
1 cup rolled oats (quick)
1 cup nuts
2 cups shredded coconut

Cream shortening and sugars.
Add slightly beaten eggs to shortening mixture.
Sift together flour, baking soda, baking powder and salt.
Add to shortening/egg mixture.
Add oats, nuts and coconut.
Might be necessary to mix by hand.
Make balls the size of walnuts.
Place on ungreased cookie sheets 2 or 3 inches apart.

Bake at 350 degrees for 12 to 15 minutes.

Easy Coconut Macaroons
Helen Salyer Perkins Johansen

2-2/3 cups coconut
4 tablespoons flour
2/3 cup sugar
¼ teaspoon salt
4 egg whites
1 teaspoon vanilla

Combine coconut, flour, sugar and salt.
Fold in egg whites and vanilla.
Mix well.
Drop by teaspoonfuls onto greased or parchment paper covered baking sheets.

Bake at 325 degrees for 18-20 minutes or until golden brown.

Cool and enjoy!

Cry Baby Cookies
Joyce Purnell (submitted by Vicki Agner Yates)

½ cup sugar
½ cup sorghum molasses
½ cup shortening
1 teaspoon soda
½ cup raisins
½ cup chopped nuts
½ cup strong coffee
1 teaspoon ginger
2-1/2 cups flour
1 teaspoon cinnamon
¼ teaspoon salt

Cream sugar and shortening.
Add sorghum molasses.
Dissolve soda in coffee and add to shortening, sugar and molasses.
Stir together flour, cinnamon, ginger and salt.
Add to liquid mixture.
Add raisins and nuts.
Drop by teaspoon onto greased cookie sheets.

Bake at 375-degrees for 15 minutes.
Cool for 5 minutes.
Remove with spatula.

Note: This is a 200 year-old recipe that came from Edith Wiseman, Crawford County, Indiana.

Jane's Cookies
Jane Allemang

1 6-ounce package chocolate bits
1 6-ounce package caramel bits
1 3-ounce can Chinese noodles
1 cup nuts

Melt chocolate and caramel bits in a saucepan over hot water. Add noodles and nuts.

Drop by spoonful onto waxed paper and cool.

Lou Sena Tolliver's Ginger Cookies
Lou Ellen Bowles Wilson

2 cups sugar
1 cup sour cream
1 cup Crisco
1 cup molasses
3-1/2 teaspoons baking soda dissolved in cream
2 eggs
Pinch of salt
1 tablespoon ginger or suit to taste
Sifted flour

Combine all ingredients except flour.
Add sifted flour to desired stiffness.
Drop onto greased cookie sheet.

Bake in a "quick oven" 12-15 minutes. (Probably 350 degrees)

Note: Grandma's cookies were always big, round and soft! She always had these cookies in her cookie jar as a special anytime treat for all of her visiting grandchildren. After she passed, I was asked if I wanted anything of hers. I immediately said, "Her cookie jar!"

I still have it sitting in a special corner on top of my kitchen cabinets.

Honey Mounds
Burline Meddock (Mrs. Steve) Tolliver

1/3 cup butter or margarine
1/3 cup sugar
1 egg
2/3 cup honey
1 teaspoon vanilla
2-1/2 cups flour
1 teaspoon baking soda
½ teaspoon salt

Cream butter, sugar, egg and honey.
Add vanilla and mix.
Add flour, salt and soda.
Mix well.

Cover in a bowl and chill at least 1 hour. This will let the dough be not as sticky to handle.
Roll into 1-inch balls and place on lightly greased or sprayed cookie sheet.
Roll in colored sugar if desired.

Bake at 350 degrees for 30 to 35 minutes until good and brown.

Author's Note: According to daughter Linda, the children were older when their mother started making the Honey Mounds. They were so good when she rolled them in red and green sugar—and very pretty for Christmas. Linda said this was a special cookie for Burline's Grandson Brian. He loved them and when her Mom knew he was coming, she would make them for him. Brian was absolutely crazy for these cookies, and he now enjoys making them with his grandsons.

Mexican Wedding Cookies
Ruby Tolliver Brewster

½ cup margarine
½ cup Crisco
1 teaspoon vanilla
¾ cup chopped nuts
2 cups flour

Cream shortening and margarine.
Add flour and nuts.
Roll into balls.

Bake 20 minutes at 325 degrees.

Roll in powdered sugar when cool.

Nut Horns
Pina Bartos & Ruby Tolliver Brewster

1 lb. margarine, softened
1 lb. cream cheese, softened
4 egg yolks
5 cups flour
Dash of salt

Mix all ingredients until smooth.
Shape into walnut-sized balls.
Chill, covered, overnight.
Roll on floured surface into 3-1/2 inch circles.

1-1/4 lb. ground nuts
2 cups milk
3 cups sugar
2 egg whites, beaten

Cook milk, nuts and sugar until thick, stirring constantly.
Spread 1 teaspoon on each circle.
Roll as for jelly roll.
Brush with egg white.

Bake on greased cookie sheet at 350 degrees for 15-20 minutes until they just start to turn light brown.
Roll warm cookies in powdered sugar.

Nut Rolls
Jean McMurdo Atkinson

1 lb. margarine
1 lb. cream cheese
1 whole egg
2 egg yolks (save whites in another bowl)
6 cups flour

Mix softened margarine and cream cheese.
Add egg and yolks.
Mix well.
Add 6 cups of flour gradually and work in.
Shape into loaf, wrap in waxed paper and refrigerate overnight.

Cut loaf in pieces and roll out in powdered sugar to 1/8 inch thick.

Cut in squares.

Filling:

3 egg whites (beaten with fork)
1-1/2 lbs. chopped nuts
¾ cup sugar
¼ cup milk

Combine all ingredients.

If too thick, add milk.

Spread thin layer of filling on pastry squares.

Roll up and then roll in powdered sugar.
Place cut side down on ungreased cookie sheet.

Bake 15 minute at 375 degrees.

Nut Rolls (cont'd)

Remove from sheet immediately and place on tea towel or rack to cool.
Can be stored in large tin container with pillow case inside as a liner.

This recipe came from the Author's very good friend from Pittsburgh, Pennsylvania.

BIG Nut Rolls
Jean McMurdo Atkinson

Dough:
8 cups flour
¼ lb. margarine
1 cup sugar
2 eggs
1-1/2 packages yeast
1-1/2 cups lukewarm milk
1 tablespoon baking powder

Dissolve yeast in ½ cup of the lukewarm milk.
Add vinegar as directed on the back of the yeast package.
Combine all ingredients.
Knead dough in a large bowl until soft – approximately 10 minutes.

I DO NOT use a mixer.
REFRIGERATE OVERIGHT

Nut Mixture:
½ teaspoon vanilla
3 lb. nuts, finely chopped
9 tablespoons honey
2 cups powdered sugar
2 cups scalded milk

Combine all ingredients.

Put dough on floured counter and cut into 4 or 5 pieces.
Roll out each of the pieces, using much flour.
After rolling out one piece, spread the nut mixture on the whole piece and then roll up like a long jelly roll.
Wrap in waxed paper and place on a cookie sheet.
I only put 2 rolls on a cookie sheet.

BIG Nut Rolls (cont'd)

After all of the 4 or 5 rolls are filled and on the cookie sheet, lay a couple of dish towels over each tray to keep them warm.
Allow rolls to raise on the counter or stove.
Let them raise for no longer than 1-1/2 hours.
After 1-1/2 hours, beat 3 egg yolks with a fork.
Brush on top and sides of each roll.
Cut about 3 slits crosswise or diagonally in the top of each roll.

Bake at 375 degrees for 40 to 45 minutes until brown.
You will have 4 or 5 large nut rolls.
You can make them bigger if you want 2 or 3 rolls.
I usually lay aluminum foil over the nut roll as they bake so they don't get too dark.
Take it off about 5 minutes before they are done.

Harry's Oatmeal Cookies
Lou Ellen Bowles Wilson

½ cup shortening
1 cup sugar
1 egg
1-3/4 cups flour
½ teaspoon baking powder
1 teaspoon baking soda
1 teaspoon cinnamon
½ teaspoon cloves
½ teaspoon nutmeg
½ - 1 cup seedless raisins
1 cup oats
1 cup applesauce
Nuts or chocolate chips (optional – or both, if desired)

Cream shortening and sugar.
Beat in egg.
Combine all dry ingredients except oats.
Combine shortening, sugar, egg mixture and dry ingredient mixture.
Mix in oats, raisins and applesauce.
Can double recipe, if desired.

Drop by spoonful onto greased or sprayed cookie sheet.
Grease or spray cookie sheet between batches.
This is a soft cookie and will spread out on cookie sheet.
Bake at 375 degrees for 10-12 minutes or until cookies are light brown.

Note: This recipe was given to Lou Ellen (Opal Tolliver Bowles Ruble's daughter) by Harry Sweet's sister-in-law, Ann Vincent. Ann was a special friend of Lou Ellen. This recipe is the favorite cookie recipe of Lou Ellen's son, Timothy Wilson.

Oatmeal Crisps
Mary Richardson

1 cup shortening
1 cup brown sugar
1 cup white sugar
2 eggs
1 teaspoon vanilla
1-1/2 cups sifted flour
1 teaspoon salt
1 teaspoon baking soda
3 cups quick oats
½ cup nuts

Cream shortening and sugar.
Add eggs and vanilla.
Mix thoroughly.
Add flour sifted with salt and soda.
Add oatmeal and nuts.
Form into three rolls 3 inches in diameter.
Wrap in waxed paper and chill overnight.
Cut in 1/8-inch slices.

Place on ungreased cookie sheets and bake at 375 degrees for 10-12 minutes.

Chewy Oatmeal Cookie
Joyce Bessenger

¾ cup butter-flavored Crisco
1-1/4 cups light brown sugar, firmly packed
1 egg
1/3 cup milk
1-1/2 teaspoons vanilla
3 cups oats, quick or old fashioned
1 cup all-purpose flour
½ teaspoon baking soda
½ teaspoon salt
¼ teaspoon cinnamon
1 cup raisins
1 cup nuts, coarsely chopped

Heat oven to 375 degrees.
Grease baking sheet with butter-flavored Crisco.
Combine Crisco, light brown sugar, egg, milk and vanilla in large bowl.
Beat at medium speed on mixer until well blended.
In separate bowl, combine oats, flour, baking soda, salt and cinnamon.
Mix into creamed mixture at low speed just until blended.
Stir in raisins and nuts.
Drop by rounded tablespoonfuls onto baking sheet, 2 inches apart.

Bake at 375 degrees for 10-12 minutes or until lightly browned.
Cool 2 minutes on baking sheet.
Remove to cooling rack.

Makes 2-1/2 dozen.

Vanishing Oatmeal Raisin Cookies
From the Quaker® Oats Box Top

½ lb. (2 sticks) margarine or butter, softened
1 cup firmly packed brown sugar
½ cup granulated sugar
2 eggs
1 teaspoon vanilla
1-1/2 cups all-purpose flour
1 teaspoon baking soda
1 teaspoon cinnamon
½ teaspoon salt (optional)
3 cups Quaker® Oats (quick or old fashioned, uncooked)
1 cup raisins

Heat oven to 350 degrees.
Beat together margarine and sugars until creamy.
Add eggs and vanilla; beat well.
Add combined flour, baking soda, cinnamon and salt; mix well.
Stir in oats and raisins; mix well.
Drop by rounded tablespoonfuls onto ungreased cookie sheet.
Bake 10 to 12 minutes or until golden brown.
Cool 1 minute on cookie sheet; remove to wire rack.

Yield: About 4 dozen

Bar Cookies: Spread dough in ungreased 13 x 9-inch metal baking pan and bake 30 to 35 minutes. Cut into bars when cool.

For high altitude, increase flour to 1-3/4 cups.

Pizzelles – an Italian Waffle Cookie
Willa Tolliver Salyer Lyons

3 eggs, beaten
¾ cup sugar
¾ cup margarine, melted
1 cup flour
1 teaspoon baking powder
¼ teaspoon salt
2 teaspoons anise flavoring
1 teaspoon vanilla

Combine all ingredients.
Spray pizzelle griddle with Pam.
Place 1 tablespoon of batter on each side of griddle.
Bake according to pizzelle griddle directions.

Note: Pizzelle's can be served as they come from the griddle, dusted with powdered sugar, or while still warm, they can be rolled into a cone and served with scoops of ice cream. Very light tasty treat!! A Pizzelle maker is very similar to an electric waffle maker with patterned metal plates. Some even come with pizzelle designs on one side and waffle design on the other.

Sugar Molasses Cookies
Edna Tolliver Hayes Hollandsworth

2 eggs
2 cups sugar
1-1/2 cups shortening
8 tablespoons molasses
½ teaspoon salt
4 cups flour
2 teaspoons cinnamon
2 teaspoons ginger
5 teaspoons soda

Beat eggs, stirring in sugar gradually.
Add shortening and molasses and beat well.
Sift together dry ingredients twice and add to egg, sugar, shortening, molasses mixture.
Make dough into small balls and roll in white sugar.
Lay on oiled cookie sheet about 1-1/2 inches apart.

Bake 12 minutes at 375 degrees.

Thumbprint Cookies
Rev. Jon Beck

1 cup margarine
¾ cup brown sugar
2 eggs, separated
2 teaspoons vanilla
2 cups self-rising flour
Ground nuts
1 can cream cheese frosting

Mix sugar, egg yolks, margarine and vanilla.
Add flour and mix well.
Dip hands into flour and form dough into balls.
Beat egg whites until foamy.
Dip dough balls in egg whites, then roll in ground nuts.

Bake 5 minutes at 375 degrees on a greased pan.
Remove from oven and make thumb prints in tops of cookies.
Bake another 5 minutes.
Cool.
Put cream cheese frosting in thumbprint.

Notes:

DRINKS

Christmas Tea
Joan Neuenschwander Schug

½ cup instant tea
1-1/2 cups sugar
14-ounce Tang
6-ounce instant lemonade
½ teaspoon cloves
1 teaspoon cinnamon

Mix all ingredients and store in tightly covered container.

Place 1-2 tablespoons (or to taste) in a mug and add boiling water. Stir to dissolve.

Mel's Wine
Isabel Gumm

20 lbs. whole grapes
10 lbs. sugar
6 quarts boiling water

Mix and let stand for 2 weeks.
Stir every day with a wooden spoon or stick.
Strain mixture.
Let mixture stand at room temperature, undisturbed, for 10 days.
Ladle off and bottle.

White Milk Punch
Priscilla Pyles Huff

2 quarts whole milk
2 quarts ginger ale
1 quart pineapple sherbet or any white sherbet
1 quart vanilla ice cream

Soften sherbet and ice cream in a punch bowl.

Add ginger ale and milk.

Mix.

Can float some ice cream on top if desired.

Makes 40 servings.

Note: This excellent punch was served at Hans & Helen Johansen's wedding reception!

Strawberry Smoothie
Helen Salyer Perkins Johansen

½ cup fresh or frozen strawberries
½ cup almond milk
4 ounces cream cheese
¼ teaspoon strawberry extract
Splenda or your choice of artificial sweetener, to taste
Ice

Place all ingredients except ice in a blender.
Blend, adding ice until smoothie is thick.

If using frozen strawberries, run blender for a bit before adding ice.

Other berries, peaches and/or bananas can be used for variety.

Great breakfast drink!

Notes:

JAMS & JELLIES

Apple Butter
Willa Tolliver Salyer Lyons

8 quarts apples
Sugar to taste
Cinnamon to taste

Cut apples in quarters or eighths – do not need to peel or core.
Put in large pan and fill ½ full of water.
Bring to a boil and cook slowly til apples are mushy, stirring occasionally.
Note: Winesaps are best for flavor.
Pour apples into food mill, two cups at a time, and process through mill, dumping peels, etc. each time.
Put in large roasting pan, sweeten and add cinnamon to taste.
Cook in 350-degree oven until apples boil.
Turn oven down to 250 degrees.
Cook for approximately 5 hours, stirring occasionally.
Apples will turn dark and thicken.
Apple butter will appear "glossy" when it is done.

While apples are cooking wash and rinse thoroughly several pint jars.
Place flat part of double lids in boiling water and continue boiling slowly.
Pour apple butter in jars.
Place flat and ring on jars and tighten as tight as you can.
As lids cool, they will "pop". That means they sealed well.

Tolliver Apple Butter
Ulis & Mary Tolliver

(Note: Following is an article written by Terry Young, Valley Post Staff Reporter, relaying the story of the Tolliver Apple Butter the family makes at the annual Corn Festival in Wilmington, Ohio.)

Mary Tolliver hasn't always made apple butter. It just seems that way. For nearly 40 years, cauldrons at the Tolliver residence have turned bushels of apples into apple butter that would grace any piece of toast or muffin.

It takes Mary a minute to remember when she turned out her first batch. "It was back during the Depression," she says. "There wasn't much to live on and you needed something to spread on that bread." So, Mary and a neighbor pooled their meager resources to whip up some apple butter. They went to a nearby orchard and picked up bagfuls of apples off the ground. Their first attempt was successful. "It was good, but then we were glad to get anything," she says.

Since the first batch, the economy may have had its ups and downs, but even inflation can't change Tolliver apple butter. The spread, which can be used in place of jelly, is an alternative use for apples—in case there are any left after the apple pies, cider and sauce are made.

"For some reason, apple butter tastes better if it is made outside," Mary says. Every year or so, Mary and husband, Ulis, drag out the old brass kettle. "The kids are all grown now, and we don't need the amount we used to," Mary says. So a hearty batch lasts the couple for several seasons. There is no written recipe for Tolliver apple butter. The product comes from no secret formula handed down from ancestors. It is, by Mary's account, a "grab and snatch" recipe. "You keep adding and tasting until you got it right for your own taste," she says.

Tolliver Apple Butter (cont'd)

In a 15-gallon brass kettle, the Tollivers can simmer up some 95 pints of apple butter using four bushels of apples. Ulis pours in a gallon of water and begins pouring in the apples as the kettle heats over the open flame. While the Tollivers generally prefer several varieties of apples, they say McIntosh apples cook up the easiest. "When they (the McIntoshs) heat up they just fall into pieces," she says.

The apples are first cored and peeled and then emptied into the kettle. As they cook down, more are poured in until the full four bushels are used. Rather than adding more water to liquefy the mixture, the Tollivers add a gallon of apple cider. "The cider is more flavorable than water," Mary says. Then as the mixture thins out, sugar is added. The Tollivers stick 25 to 30 pounds of sugar into their mixture. A sampling every now and then tells the cook if the butter is sweet enough. As the mixture begins to stiffen, two nine-and-one-half-ounce bags of cinnamon beans and a single teaspoon of cinnamon oil are added.

The mixture requires almost constant stirring until it's thick enough for "jarring." When Ulis is asked about the apple butter making, he offers a few comments and refers all other question to his wife. "I just help stir," Ulis says. He also helps with the eating.

Author's Note: Obviously, this recipe makes more than any family would want to make, but the Tolliver family currently makes this large quantity and sells it every year in September at the annual Corn Festival in Wilmington, Ohio. Proceeds from the apple butter sales go to fund a scholarship for a Wilmington High School senior who is planning a farming related career.

MEAT, POULTRY & SEAFOOD

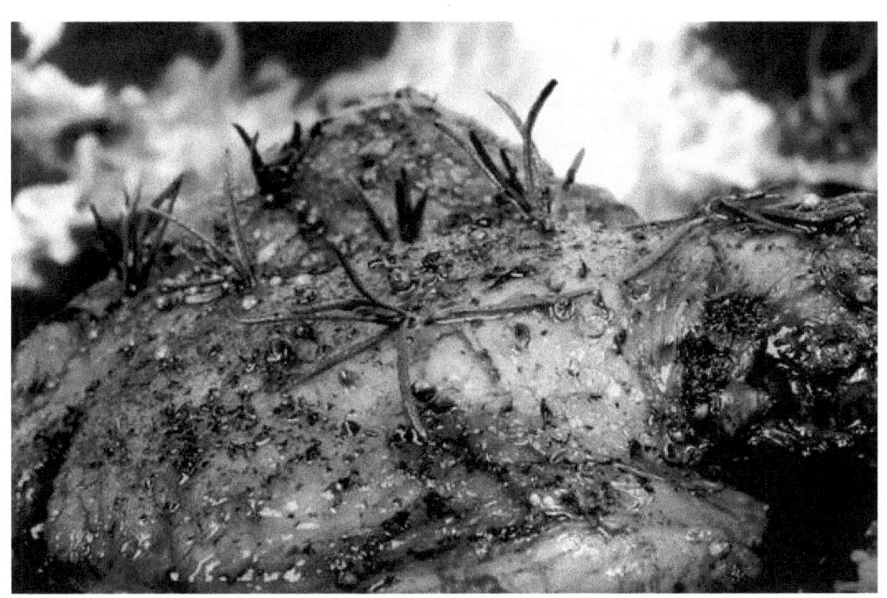

Freezing Bacon
Edna Tolliver Hayes Hollandsworth

Bacon and other meat can be frozen between wax paper and in bread bags.
For bacon, take a long strip of wax paper on table and start in center of paper.
Lay on a strip of bacon, fold paper, then another strip of bacon and fold paper till you use this half of paper.
Turn the stack of bacon over and use other half of paper till all is between paper.

Keeps well and easy to use as needed – one piece or 6 or whatever!

Beef Brisket
Gary Perkins

4-pound beef brisket, flat half
1 large onion, diced
1 can mushroom caps
1 clove garlic, crushed
1 tablespoon olive oil
Salt and pepper to taste

Cut a pocket horizontally in the beef brisket.
Stuff with onions, mushrooms and garlic.
Close pocket with toothpicks.

Rub brisket with salt, pepper and olive oil.

Brown on both sides on the grill.

Place in covered baking dish and bake at 200 degrees for 5 hours.

Beef Marinade

Greg & Kim Evans
Crossroads Family Restaurant & Gift Shop
615 West Highway 50
Versailles, IN   47042

1 quart apple cider
1-1/3 cups Worcestershire sauce
2 teaspoons garlic powder
2/3 teaspoon chili powder
1-1/3 tablespoons Lowry's Seasoning Salt
5 lbs. beef sirloin

Mix first 5 ingredients thoroughly.

Pour over meat and refrigerate overnight.

Beef Stew
Priscilla Pyles Huff

1 pound stew beef
1 tablespoon flour
1 teaspoon salt
1 tablespoon oil
1 onion, cut in quarters
2 small potatoes, cut in quarters
½ green pepper, cut in quarters
1 stalk celery, cut in 1-inch pieces
8 baby carrots
1 4-ounce can sliced mushrooms

Flour beef and brown in oil.
Add salt, onion, potatoes, pepper, celery, carrots and mushrooms.

Pour into baking dish.

Add 1-1/4 cups water and cover.

Bake at 350 degrees for 2 hours, stirring occasionally.

Pressure Cooker Beef Stew
Helen Salyer Perkins Johansen

1 tablespoon oil
1 lb. beef, cubed in 1-inch squares
1 large onion, sliced
Salt and pepper, to taste
½ cup water
4 small potatoes
4 small carrots
1 tablespoon flour
¼ cup water

Heat pressure cooker and add oil.
Brown meat in the cooker.
Add onion, salt, pepper and ½ cup water.
Place small potatoes and carrots over the meat.
Other vegetables can be added if you choose.
Close cover securely.
Place Pressure Regulator on vent pipe and cook 10 to 12 minutes with Pressure Regulator rocking slowly.
Cool Cooker at once.
Make a paste of the flour and ¼ cup water and stir into stew to thicken.

Another method of preparing stew is to cook the meat separately for 8-10 minutes, then add the vegetables and cook 5 minutes with Pressure Regulator rocking slowly.

Note: I have made this stew in my pressure cooker for years and just love it. When cooking in a pressure cooker, you must be extremely careful that you don't get in the path of the steam when it is cooking or releasing. There are many newer cookers available but I still like to use my old Presto Pressure Cooker for beef stew!

Beef Stroganoff
Karen Tolliver Kratzer

Left-over steak or meat of choice
1 package onion soup mix
1 small container sour cream
2 cans cream of mushroom soup
Noodles of choice, cooked

Combine meat, onion soup mix, sour cream and mushroom soup in saucepan.
Heat on "Low" until near boiling.

Serve over cooked noodles.

Chicken and Rice
Linda Tolliver Richard

1 9-ounce package Vigo Saffron Yellow Rice
3 chicken leg quarters

Boil chicken until tender.
Cool and remove skin.
Shred chicken.
Cook rice in chicken broth, adding more water as desired.
Rice already has all the flavoring in it.
Cook til rice is tender.
Combine rice and shredded chicken.

Serve while hot!

Chicken Parisienne
Hans Johansen, Jr.

8 pieces chicken breast halves
3 tablespoons butter or margarine
1 small onion, sliced
1 cup sour cream
1 cup mushrooms, sliced
1 can (10-3/4 ounces) cream of chicken soup
¾ cup Holiday House Sherry cooking wine
Salt and pepper to taste

Season breasts with salt and pepper.
Melt butter or margarine in skillet or frying pan.
Brown chicken on both sides and steam on low heat until tender.
Arrange chicken, onion and mushrooms in a casserole or baking pan.
Mix remaining ingredients together in a separate bowl.
Pour over chicken.

Bake in 400-degree oven for 45 to 50 minutes.

Baked Chicken
Edna Tolliver Hays Hollandsworth

1 medium fryer chicken
1-1/2 cups corn flakes (or other flake cereal)
1 egg
¼ cup milk
¼ cup flour
1/8 teaspoon salt
Dash pepper
1-1/2 tablespoons margarine or butter, melted
1/8 teaspoon sage (optional)
3 tablespoons parmesan cheese (optional)

Cut chicken into serving pieces. Dry pieces with paper towel.

Crush corn flakes or other flake cereal to make at least ¾ cups after crushing.

Beat egg and milk slightly.
Add flour, salt and pepper.
Add sage and cheese, if desired.
Beat until smooth.

Dip chicken pieces in egg mixture and coat with cereal.

Place single layer of chicken, skin side up, on a greased or foil-lined shallow pan.

Drizzle with butter.

Bake uncovered at 350 degrees about 45 minutes or until done and golden brown.
Do not turn pieces.
Drumsticks and thighs are great for this recipe.

Baked Chicken (cont'd)

Author's Note: This was one of Daughter Audrey's favorite recipes, along with homemade bread and green beans her Mother had grown in her garden and canned. They had plenty of canned fruits and vegetables all year around. They had apple trees and Aunt Edna would make and can apple pie filling. She could make a meal and apple pie any time anyone came to their home. Audrey said it was rare that they didn't have someone eating with them or staying with them.

Crunchy Fried Chicken
Edna Tolliver Hayes Hollandsworth

1 medium-sized fryer chicken
Oil
Flour
Buttermilk
Salt and pepper

Cut chicken into serving pieces.
Heat ½ inch deep oil in electric skillet to 300 degrees.
Dip chicken in flour, then in buttermilk and back in flour to coat well.
Place in hot oil till space is full, but not crowded or stacked on other pieces.
Salt and pepper to taste.
Cover and cook at 300 degrees until edges are getting golden brown.
Turn only once, brown the other side.
Chicken will be done when brown on both sides if skillet is right temperature.

I strain off oil when I take chicken out, leaving some for gravy with the crumbles.
In covered jar, oil will keep well in refrigerator for long periods for next frying of chicken.
Add a small amount more of oil each new frying.

This chicken will warm over well.
I cook a large skillet full and warm in oven on low heat for another meal.

Serves:
3 boys and little girl, Sue. Maybe some left!

Lemon Chicken Barbeque
Hans Johansen, Jr.

1 cup salad oil
1-1/2 cups lemon juice
½ cup water
3 tablespoons salt
6 tablespoons sugar
3 teaspoons Tabasco sauce
1 teaspoon dry mustard
2 teaspoons Worcestershire sauce
2 lb. chicken thighs without skin

Heat all ingredients except chicken in a heavy saucepan.
Keep hot for basting.
Dip chicken in sauce and place over low charcoal fire.
Baste chicken and turn every ten minutes.
Approximately 1-hour cooking time required.

If cooking in an oven broiler, set oven temperature about 350 degrees.
Broil as suggested for charcoal, turning frequently and basting each turn.
Turn temperature down if chicken browns too quickly.

If cooking on a Weber grill, turn burners to "High" and place chicken pieces over hot burners to sear in juices.
Turn pieces over after 3-4 minutes.
When both sides are seared, turn front burner to "Low" and rear burner "Off".

Place pieces over middle and back area after dipping into sauce.
Re-dip and turn pieces over every 10 minutes until done.

Lemon Chicken Barbeque (cont'd)

An alternate choice that reduces burning is to place aluminum foil on top of the grill piercing it often between the grate bars to allow drippings to escape.
Place chicken on top of aluminum foil and cook as noted above.
Total cooking time is approximately 1 hour.

Mediterranean Chicken
Priscilla Pyles Huff

1 chicken, cut-up, or
4 chicken breasts, or
8 chicken legs
½ lb. button mushrooms, sliced
1 onion, sliced thin
1 green pepper, sliced thin
1 16-ounce can tomatoes, broken up
2 garlic cloves, minced
½ cup raw rice
4 tablespoons olive oil
¼ cup flour
1 teaspoon salt
1 teaspoon Italian seasoning
1/8 teaspoon ground red pepper
1 cup water

Dredge chicken in flour.
Shake off excess.
Heat oil in very large skillet.
Add chicken and brown.
Remove from skillet.
Sauté garlic a few seconds.
Add mushrooms, onion and green pepper.
Sauté 5 minutes.
Stir in tomatoes, water, salt, Italian seasoning and pepper.
Bring to a boil.
Stir in rice.
Return chicken to skillet, cover and simmer 45 minutes.

Cream Roasted Chicken
Edna Tolliver Hayes Hollandsworth

1 medium-size frying chicken
1 stick butter or margarine
Flour
Salt and pepper, to taste
1 large can evaporated milk

Cut chicken into serving pieces.
Melt butter in roaster pan.
Roll chicken pieces in flour and arrange in buttered pan, one layer only.
Salt and pepper to taste.
Place in hot oven (about 425 degrees) uncovered until chicken starts to brown on edges and on top.

Heat evaporated milk and pour over chicken evenly.
Cover and return to oven on high heat until milk gets bubbly or boiling.
Then reduce heat to about 350 degrees.
Bake until tender and brown but not dry.
Can be left in oven on very lowest heat until ready to serve.
Remove from pan to platter and make milk gravy in the goodies in the pan.

Make plenty of gravy for hungry husband and boys!

Party Chicken
Gladys Hamilton Green

8 chicken breasts
Sliced ham
Bacon
1 can mushroom soup, undiluted
½ pint sour cream

Wrap ham around the chicken breast.
Wrap ½ slice bacon over the ham.
Use toothpick to hold the bacon and ham on the chicken.
Place chicken in a 9x13 baking pan.
Combine mushroom soup and sour cream.
Pour soup mixture over the chicken.

Bake at 275 degrees for 3 hours.

Gerri's Chicken Pot Pie
Geraldine Green Miracle

2 cans chicken (I use the 13-ounce cans from Sam's)
1 family size package of frozen mixed vegetables
2 cans of whole potatoes, diced
1 can corn
¾ cup fresh carrots, sliced
1 large Vidalia onion, diced
1 can cream of chicken soup
1 can cream of mushroom soup
1 can cream of celery soup (all soups are Campbell's)
1 cup of frozen peas, if desired
2 two-crust pie pastries

In a large bowl, mix everything together.

Prepare the crust and place mixture in crust. I usually use Old Sister Schubert Roll pans to bake the pies in or some deep pie pan or baking dish.

Top with another crust and cut vent holes in the top crust.

Bake at 350 degrees for about an hour or until golden brown on top.

This recipe will make 2 large pies. I usually make it and give one to someone and have one for dinner!

If the mixture seems dry, I will add another can of cream of mushroom soup.

Enjoy!!

Chicken Salad
Priscilla Pyles Huff

6 frozen chicken tenders, cooked and shredded
3 stalks celery, chopped
½ cup mayonnaise
1 tablespoon lemon juice
2 teaspoons Dijon mustard – prefer Grey Poupon
Salt and pepper

Mix mayonnaise, lemon juice and mustard together.

Mix in chicken and celery.

Season with salt and pepper to taste.

Chill before serving.

Author's Note: The following article is one I did for a writing class many years ago. It describes the process by which I received a recipe for frying chicken and is the main dish of our families' favorite dinner.

"NOBODY FRIES CHICKEN LIKE YOU, MOM."

My family is totally spoiled when it comes to chicken! Well, let's face it, they are totally spoiled when it comes to a lot of things. They are particularly spoiled when it comes to fried chicken. If "The Colonel" depended on our purchases to survive, he'd be bankrupt! Many times my sons have come home with the lament, "Nobody fries chicken like you, Mom." I'm extremely flattered by their enthusiasm. However, when I'm standing over a hot skillet of chicken on an equally hot July day, I question my sanity in ever frying that first piece!

My talent for creating this highly praised delicacy was acquired in the early 60's at the "Chicken Inn" in Chillicothe, Ohio. When my date informed me that we would be enjoying the best fried chicken in the world on Tuesday night, I smugly reminded him he had never tasted my fried chicken! Hadn't I been taught at an early age that the way to a man's heart was through his stomach! Later that evening, if I hadn't been so stuffed, I would have gladly eaten my words. It was fabulous! The tender pieces of chicken, snugly wrapped in a golden brown crust, had a very unusual taste. An entire half of a chicken disappeared from my plate in record time!

We became such regular chicken eaters that the older couple who owned the restaurant began stopping by our table to chat. "This is the best chicken I have ever tasted," I complimented. "How in the world do you fry it?" I queried. I was really surprised when, with a smile, he slid into the booth beside me and began explaining his secret! Was he smiling because I asked for his recipe, or was he just relieved to get off his tired feet for a few minutes? I now realize the smile that generates from getting off tired, chicken-frying feet!

"Well now, young lady," he started, "the most important thing is to use a heavy skillet. The next most important thing is don't get in a hurry! Fill the skillet nearly half full of cooking oil and let it heat slowly." He had my full attention! He was actually going through a detailed explanation. Sharing his expertise seemed as exciting to him as it was to me.

"Make sure your chicken is fresh," he warned, "and select smaller chickens. They fry up a lot better." All of this was pretty much the same advice my Mom and Betty Crocker had shared. When was he going to come up with some unusual ingredient or method! With eager anticipation, I revved up my memory bank. Somehow, I felt it wouldn't be proper to pull out a pencil and paper. Didn't want him to think I was going to open my own "Chicken Inn."

Slowly he continued. "Now, while the oil is heating, measure out about 2-3 cups of flour in a bowl. Add a teaspoon of salt and as much pepper as you like, probably about a teaspoon. Also, add a teaspoon of paprika. This gives the chicken it's golden brown look." There it was! The secret ingredient! (I later found out paprika was only part of the secret.) "Mix the salt, pepper and paprika real well," he instructed, "and then in another bowl, mix two beaten eggs, a cup of milk, and half teaspoon of salt. Now you're ready to start frying! Dip the chicken, one piece at a time, into the flour mixture, then into the egg and milk mixture, and then back into the flour. Make sure to coat each piece well."

"Now, here's the real secret," he confided. "Don't put too many pieces in your skillet at one time! The pieces can touch, but crowding pieces into the skillet just doesn't work. The chicken needs space around each piece to allow for even browning. And don't skimp on the oil, either. Make sure the pieces are about half covered with oil."

"But that's not all there is to frying good chicken," he cautioned. "Put a lid on your skillet, turn the fire down low, and don't bother it for about a half an hour. Then, take off the lid, turn the chicken over and allow it to brown on the other side. And don't be flipping the pieces from side to side. That disturbs the crust. Just turn it one time."

Well, I could hardly wait to try my hand. At first, I had a tendency to "pick at" the chicken as it was frying to see if it was getting brown, but the more I prepared, the more confident I was to just leave it alone. As the years went by and my three sons came on the scene, "Mom's Fried Chicken" became at least a weekly meal, usually on Sunday. Some family member was kind enough to give me an electric skillet for Christmas one year, and it really made frying chicken so much easier. All I had to do was warm the skillet to 250 degrees while I mixed the flour and egg/milk mixtures, put the breaded chicken in, put the lid on, and turn the thermostat down to about 175-200 degrees. Wait about a half hour. Turn the chicken over. You can tell when the pieces begin to turn golden brown on the edges, they are ready to turn. Then I leave the lid off, and when all of the edges of a piece are brown, I take that piece up. I always put a mat of paper towels on the platter to soak up the excess oil and keep the chicken crisp. When it is all done and ready for serving, I just slip the oil-soaked towels out from under the chicken, and a beautiful, finger-lickin' main dish is ready for the troops.

  One more little trick I always do is to clean the batter off my fingers periodically as I'm putting the chicken in the grease and drop the little blobs into the grease. They brown much quicker than the chicken and can be scooped out and put on the paper towels as little "goodies" to be snitched by eager fingers waiting for dinner.

  I spent many, many hours "tending my chicken" over the years. Now my sons are all married with families of their own. I only fry chicken now for special occasions or when I get especially hungry for it myself. Since the boys have been on their own, I have spent many hours on the phone giving specific directions on the art of frying chicken. Thus, the reason for this dissertation. I feel sure Ma Bell won't suffer too much from my shortened phone calls, and "The Colonel" will still be able to make a good living. My reward is knowing my extended family (and any others who come across this recipe) will bask in the glory of hearing an adoring child say, **"Nobody fries chicken like you, Mom (or Dad)! "**

Chicken Inn Fried Chicken

Helen Salyer Perkins Johansen

Flour Mixture:

4-6 boneless chicken breasts
3 cups flour
2 teaspoons salt
1 teaspoon black pepper
1-1/2 teaspoons paprika

Egg/Milk Mixture:

3 eggs, beaten with fork
2 cups milk
1 teaspoon salt

Fill electric skillet nearly half full of cooking oil and heat to 250 degrees.
While oil is heating, combine Flour Mixture ingredients in one bowl and Egg/Milk Mixture in another.
Rinse chicken in cool water and cut in half or chunks if desired. (Mixed chicken parts can also be used.)
Dip the chicken, one piece at a time, into the Flour Mixture, then into the Egg/Milk Mixture, and then back into the Flour Mixture, making sure to coat each piece well.
Place coated chicken into the hot oil, again one piece at a time as they are coated.
Leave space between each piece to allow for even browning.
As pieces are being dipped, periodically clean batter from fingers and drop into skillet to make delicious little "goodies".

When all pieces are coated and in skillet, put lid on skillet (close vent on lid) and turn thermostat down to 175 degrees.
Allow chicken to cook one half hour.
Do not disturb pieces during this time.
Remove lid.

Chicken Inn Fried Chicken (cont'd)

If chicken is golden brown on the bottom and a portion of the side, carefully turn each piece over and allow it to brown on the other side.
If not sufficiently brown on the bottom, allow chicken to cook another 5-10 minutes with lid off before turning.

Do not disturb pieces any more than necessary as this causes the crust to break off.

After turning, leave the lid off and continue cooking for another 30 minutes or until golden brown.
As each piece browns, remove it and place it on a platter covered with a thick mat of paper towels to soak up the excess oil and keep the chicken crisp.
The "goodies" will brown quicker than the chicken - remove them as soon as they are brown.
When all pieces are finished, slip the oil-soaked towels out from under the chicken, and serve while piping hot.

Cornish Hens
Priscilla Pyles Huff

1 Cornish hen, thawed and cut in half
1 tablespoon oil
½ teaspoon salt
1 teaspoon paprika
1 teaspoon poultry seasoning
¼ teaspoon pepper

Combine oil, salt, paprika, poultry seasoning and pepper.

Rub hen with oil mixture.

Place skin-side up on rack in a baking pan.

Bake at 350 degrees for 1 hour and 15 minutes.

Makes 2 servings.

Alice's Cube Steak and Gravy
Alice Ogez Litzy Perkins

6 cube steaks
Flour
Vegetable oil
Lipton Beefy Onion Soup Mix

Wash and pat dry cube steaks.
Dredge in flour and fry steaks in vegetable oil.
Just cook steaks until flour begins to brown.
Remove steaks and place in large glass baking dish.

Mix 1 or 2 packs soup mix, depending on how big steaks are, with 1 cup cold water to dissolve.
Once mix is completely dissolved pour over steaks.
You can use any of the Lipton soup mixes, Mushroom/Onion or Onion.
Do not add extra salt and pepper when breading.

Add enough cold water to completely cover steaks.
Completely seal baking dish with aluminum foil.

Bake at 350 degrees for 90 minutes.
Check at 60 minutes, you want steaks to be very tender and gravy to thicken.

Do not overcook as gravy will dry up.

Enchiladas
Dorcas Neidig

Tortillas:
1 cup flour
1 cup corn meal
Salt
Water

Combine all ingredients and add enough water to make a thin batter, 2 cups or more.
Fry as you would a pancake.
Always keep batter thin.

Filling:
2 lb. hamburger
1 large onion
Velveeta cheese, sliced

Brown hamburger and onion.
Place hamburger on tortillas and cover with a slice of Velveeta cheese.
Roll the tortillas up and place in a baking pan or dish.

Sauce:
1 can hot enchilada sauce
1 can tomato soup
1 can water

Mix all ingredients and pour over enchiladas.
Bake at 350 degrees for 30 minutes.

Mexican Goulash
Jessica Green Ward

2 lbs. elbow macaroni
3 lbs. ground beef
2 large cans Rotel mild salsa
Fiesta blended shredded cheese

Boil elbow macaroni until tender and drain.
Brown ground beef and drain.
Mix together macaroni, ground beef and Rotel mild salsa.

Dish up and top with Fiesta blended cheese.

Also, great with warm tortillas!

Baked Ham
Helen Salyer Perkins Johansen

Ham – with bone, ½ - ¾ lbs. per person to be served
Ham – boneless, 1/8 – ¼ lbs. per person to be served

Choose butt portion of ham if not getting a whole ham.
Place in a shallow pan with a cup or so of water underneath.
Cover tightly with foil.

Bake at 325 degrees – see timing on ham package.

Add honey, pineapple topping or glaze, if desired

DO NOT OVERCOOK!

Ham Loaf with Fruit Sauce
Bob-O-Link Restaurant
Columbus, Indiana

4 lbs. cooked or spiced ham
1 lb. celery
4 ounces onions
¼ ounce parsley
1-1/2 lbs. bread crumbs
3 eggs
12 ounces tomatoes
1 tablespoon salt
½ teaspoon ground pepper

Finely chop ham, celery, onions and parsley.
Add bread crumbs, eggs, tomatoes, salt and pepper.
Place in oiled bread pans.
Bake at 375 degrees for 30 minutes.

Fruit Sauce:

8 ounces brown sugar
1 teaspoon dry mustard
1 teaspoon cinnamon
½ ounce vinegar
12 ounces crushed pineapple

Mix brown sugar, dry mustard, cinnamon, vinegar and pineapple in bowl.
Spread over loaves.

Bake loaves another 45 minutes.

Ham Loaf with Fruit Sauce (cont'd)

Heat the fruit sauce.
Serve 4 ounces of ham and 1 ounce of sauce.
Takes 1-1/2 hours to cook.
Prepare the previous night.

Note: This recipe is for 25 people. It was served at the Bob-O-Link Restaurant at 25th Street and National Road in Columbus, Indiana from 1947 until 1967.

Tender Juicy Hamburgers
Edna Tolliver Hayes Hollandsworth

Make a hole in center of hamburgers before frying or freezing.
Add your favorite seasoning when frying.
Center will be done before edges get too dry.

The frozen ones will thaw more quickly also with hole in the center.

I buy large amount when I get a good buy and mold them with the hole in the center and place between wax paper and then in freezer bag.

You can take out one or as many as you need.

Put them on a wire rack and turn a fan on them for quick thaw.

It keeps them tender not to thaw in hot skillet.

Mexican Lasagna
Jayme Hartwell

Ingredients:

1-2 lbs. ground beef
1 jar of salsa, any type
1 jar of traditional spaghetti sauce (i.e. Not Meat Sauce)
Flour tortillas (4 large or 6 small)
2 packages shredded cheese, any type (Mexican or 4 Cheese)

Brown and drain ground beef.
Mix salsa and spaghetti sauce together.
Put ½ of sauce mixture in bottom of 9 x 13 pan.
Top with one layer of tortillas (you can tear the tortillas to fit the pan and use the torn off parts to fill in the corners).
Spread another ¼ of the sauce on tortillas.
Spread ½ the crumbled beef on top and then sprinkle with one package of shredded cheese.
Repeat the layers - sauce, tortillas, sauce, beef and cheese.

Bake in oven at 350 degrees for 30-35 minutes until heated through and cheese is bubbly.
The leftovers freeze very well.

Chicken can be substituted for the beef and wheat tortillas can be used instead of flour tortillas. Reduces the carbs and calories.

Ann Jones' Meat Loaf
Norma Jones Dalton

1-1/2 lbs. lean ground beef
1 can tomato juice
¾ cups Quaker® Oats
2 eggs, slightly beaten
¼ cup chopped onion
½ cup chopped green pepper
½ teaspoon salt
¼ teaspoon pepper

Heat oven to 350 degrees.

Combine all ingredients and mix thoroughly.
Press into 8x4 inch loaf pan.
Put ketchup on top.

Bake one hour.
Drain and bake 15 minutes.

Let stand 5 minutes before serving.

Meat Loaf Supreme
Hans Johansen, Jr.

1 envelope Lipton Recipe Secrets Beefy Onion Soup Mix
2 lbs. ground beef
¾ cup Quaker® Oats "1 Minute"
2 whole eggs
¾ cup water
1/3 cup ketchup

Preheat oven to 350 degrees.

In a large bowl, combine all ingredients.
Pour mixture into a 9x13 baking pan and shape into a loaf.
Can use a large bread loaf pan.

Bake uncovered 1 hour or until done.

Let stand 10 minutes before serving.

Muffin Pan Meat Loaves
Jayme Hartwell

Start to Finish 30 minutes   6 servings

2 eggs, lightly beaten
¾ cup shredded Mexican cheese blend
1 tablespoon each chili powder and Worcestershire sauce
2 garlic cloves, minced
1-1/2 teaspoons hot pepper sauce
1 teaspoon dried parsley flakes
½ teaspoon salt
¼ teaspoon pepper
¾ lb. lean ground beef (90% lean)
¾ lb. ground turkey

Topping:
½ cup ketchup
3 tablespoons brown sugar
1 teaspoon prepared mustard

Preheat oven to 375 degrees.
In a bowl, combine the first nine ingredients.
Add beef and turkey; mix lightly but thoroughly.
Place 1/3 cup mixture into each of 12 ungreased muffin cups, pressing lightly.

In a bowl, mix topping ingredients.
Spoon over meat loaves.

Bake, uncovered, at 350 degrees for 15-20 minutes or until a thermometer reads 165 degrees.

Muffin Pan Meat Loaves (cont'd)

FREEZING OPTIONS:

Bake meat loaves without topping.
Cool and freeze, covered, on waxed paper-lined baking sheet.
Put in freezer bags.

To use, thaw in refrigerator overnight.
Place on a greased baking pan.
Prepare topping and spread over the tops.

Bake in a preheated 350-degree oven until heated through.

Pastichio   (Greek Lasagna)
Kathy Lafakis

Cream Sauce
6 tablespoons butter
1 quart hot milk (heat in microwave 3-4 minutes)
¼ cup grated Parmesan cheese
½ cup water
¾ cup flour
2 teaspoons salt
4 eggs

Melt butter in 2-quart saucepan over medium heat.
Add flour, stirring until roux mix is golden in color.
Gradually stir in hot milk (mixture will be pasty and smooth).
Cook stirring constantly, until sauce is smooth and has thickened.
Remove from heat and cool slightly.
Stir in Parmesan cheese and salt and set aside.
When partially cool, stir in eggs (one at a time) and beat lightly.
Set aside.

Meat Filling
2 medium chopped onions
4 tablespoons butter
3 lbs. ground beef
½ cup water
4 oz of tomato paste
salt, pepper, and ground cinnamon, to taste

In large skillet, sauté onion in butter until golden brown.
Add beef and crumble.
Add cinnamon, salt and pepper.
Add water and tomato paste.
Cook for 5 minutes under medium heat.
Let cool slightly.

Pastichio (Greek Lasagna) (cont'd)

Macaroni
1 lb. large macaroni (or elbow macaroni can substitute)
¼ cup grated Parmesan cheese
4 eggs, slightly beaten

Preheat oven to 350 degrees.
Prepare pasta while meat is cooking.
Cook pasta and drain per package directions.
When the pasta is lukewarm, add eggs and Parmesan cheese. Mix well.
Add meat mixture, season as needed and add additional cheese.

Spray a 10x15x2" pan with non-stick cooking spray.
Sprinkle a fine coating of Parmesan cheese on the bottom of the pan.
Place pasta and meat in pan.
Bake 10 minutes.
Remove pan and top with cream sauce.
Sprinkle with Parmesan cheese.
Continue baking for 40-50 minutes until top is golden.
Allow to cool 10 minutes before cutting and serving.

Yields approximately 18 pieces

Hans' Pork Loin, Pork Shoulder or Beef Brisket
Hans Johansen, Jr.

Pork loin or shoulder or beef brisket
1 head of cabbage
2 large cans (49.5 ounces) chicken broth
Salt and pepper

Wash and place whole roast in pan.
Use throw away aluminum pan for easiest clean up.
Salt and pepper well.
Wash and cut up cabbage and place around the roast.
Add chicken broth.
Cover tightly with aluminum foil.
Bake in 250-degree oven until fork tender.
It will take approximately 4 – 6 hours; overnight is best.

All of these cuts of meat can be done the same way.

Pork and Orange Juice Roast
Mark Perkins

3-4 lb. pork tenderloin or shoulder roast
3 oranges
¼ teaspoon salt
1 teaspoon black pepper
6 garlic cloves, peeled and crushed
2 teaspoons oregano

Mix together juice of one orange, salt, pepper, garlic and oregano.
Let sit for 15 minutes.
Put roast into a covered baking dish.
Poke holes in the roast with a knife.
Pour orange juice mixture over top of roast and rub into holes.
Marinate for 30 minutes.

Preheat oven to 350 degrees.
Squeeze juice of a second orange around the roast in the baking dish.
Cover and bake for 2 hours.
Add water if dish gets dry.

After 2 hours, increase heat to 400 degrees.
Squeeze the juice of the last orange and use to baste the meat.
Cook for 30 to 45 minutes until meat is browned and develops a crust.

Remove from oven and let stand for 15 minutes.

Slice or pull apart and serve with white rice and spicy red beans or homemade salsa or crumble corn bread into bottom of a bowl and pour "soup beans" over top. Shred pork on top and add homemade salsa.

Pork and Orange Juice Roast (cont'd)

Homemade Salsa

2 fresh tomatoes, chopped
1 medium yellow onion, chopped
4 Jalapeno pepper rings
1 teaspoon lemon juice
½ teaspoon vegetable oil

Combine all ingredients in a bowl.
Mix thoroughly.
For a fresh garden taste, serve immediately.
Otherwise, seal in plastic bowl and chill overnight.

Variations:

Add cilantro, parsley or chili pepper to taste.

Add tomato sauce for a salsa that is more like jar salsa.

Potomac Grilled Oysters
Earl Gill

The Oyster, mother nature's most perfect treat. I've heard this comment a million times. Imagine the first person who pulled what resembled a rock from the bottom of the bay and decided to take the first bite. I can't imagine how hungry that person must have been but I'm glad they did. Oysters have been in my diet since I was a little boy. They're good raw, steamed, fried, broiled, on a roll, or as a shooter in a shot glass but little known to people is that they are awesome grilled. Besides having their own natural serving dish, they also have some unique features. There is a bottom and top side to each oyster. Just like most people are right handed, most oysters will curve to the left when sitting on its bottom side and looking from the hinge to the top edge of the shell. Rarely will you find one that curves to the right.

Ingredients:

24 Bay Oysters (meatier oysters with a deeper shell to hold the ingredients)
Variety of shredded cheese (I prefer sharp cheddar, mozzarella, parmesan)
Real bacon bits
Tabasco sauce
Oyster knife
Insulated rubber glove for your non-dominate hand

Cooking:

Heat your grill to around 300 degrees and place your oysters bottom side down. It's the flat side or if you're not sure, remember the shell curves to the left when it's resting on its bottom and looking from the hinge to top edge.

Potomac Grilled Oysters (cont'd)

Close the grill and let them cook for about 5 minutes. As they roast, they will begin to open up. So, you can check their progress by tapping on the top shell. The shells will start clapping.
When they're done, use your gloved hand to pull the oysters off the grill and hold the oyster upside down to remove the bottom shell with the oyster knife. There is a sweet spot in the grilling process where the muscle (the tissue that holds the shell close) will easily separate from the bottom shell.
Once you get all the bottoms off, you can begin to doctor up your oysters to taste. I like to add a dash of Tabasco and some bacon followed by different cheeses.
Then return them to the grill until the cheese melts. They're ready to eat.

Some variations:

Grill the oysters naked. When done, dip the oyster in buffalo wings sauce.

Grill the oysters naked. When done, squeeze some lime juice on them and add parmesan.

Hans' Pizza
Hans Johansen, Jr.

Crust:
1 package yeast
1-1/4 cups warm water
2 tablespoons oil
2 eggs, beaten
¼ teaspoon salt
4 cups all-purpose flour

Sprinkle yeast in ¼ cup of warm water.
Mix rest of water, beaten eggs and oil together.
Add salt to flour and mix together before combining with water and eggs. Add rest of ingredients and mix well till all are moistened. Knead and let rise. Punch down and place onto 2 greased pizza pans. Spread out to cover pans.

Sauce:
1 small can tomato paste
1 15-ounce can tomato sauce
1 onion, chopped and browned
1 tablespoon brown sugar
1 teaspoon oregano
Garlic salt to taste
Salt and pepper to taste
1 teaspoon dry mustard
1 teaspoon fennel seed

Bring all ingredients to boil and let simmer.
Spread on crusts and top with cooled crumbled sausage (optional), mozzarella cheese (shredded), brick cheese (shredded), sliced onions, green peppers, mushrooms and whatever!

Bake at 425 degrees for 20 minutes or until lightly browned.

Homemade Pizza
Mona Eble Plumer

Crust:

2 cups Bisquick
2 tablespoons mustard
½ cup milk

Stir mustard into milk.
Blend into Bisquick.
Put on a floured surface and knead one minute.
Roll out to fit pizza pan.
Prick surface with a fork.
Bake in 425-degree oven 5-7 minutes.
Remove from oven, reduce heat to 375 degrees.

Topping:

6 ounces tomato sauce
1 tablespoon sugar
1 tablespoon onion, chopped
2 tablespoons mustard
¼ teaspoon oregano
1 pound sausage or hamburger
2 tablespoons parmesan cheese
1 cup grated cheese (your choice)
1 cup grated mozzarella cheese

Combine first 5 ingredients and pour into a saucepan.
Bring to a boil. Turn heat to simmer and simmer for 10 minutes.
Pour onto partially baked crust.
Brown meat, drain. Sprinkle crust with cheese, meat, cheese.
Top with mozzarella.

Bake at 375 degrees for 15 minutes.

Dot's Pork Chops
Dorothy Atkinson Ristoff

4-6 lean pork chops
1 small onion, chopped
2 stalks celery, chopped
1 tablespoon yellow mustard
Handful of brown sugar
1 large can tomato sauce
Squirt of lemon juice

Brown pork chops in oil.
Combine onion, celery, mustard, brown sugar, tomato sauce and lemon juice.
Pour over pork chops in skillet.

Cover and simmer for 40 minutes or so.

Delicious!!

Pork Chops in Sour Cream
Priscilla Pyles Huff

2 pork chops, salted and peppered
¼ cup sour cream
½ onion, chopped
1 can mushroom pieces, drain and reserve liquid

Brown chops on both sides.
Cook until tender and remove from skillet.
Add onions and mushrooms in the same skillet.
Brown.
Add sour cream and mushroom liquid.
Mix well.
Add chops back into the skillet with the liquid.

Continue cooking 20 minutes.

Easy Pot Roast
Geraldine Green Miracle

Chuck Roast
1 can golden mushroom soup
1 can French onion soup
1 or 2 cans water (1 can if using crock pot; 2 cans if using oven)

Crockpot Method:

Place a liner in the crockpot, so clean up is easy.
Place pot roast in bottom.
Add both cans of soup.
Add 1 can of water.
Set crockpot on low and cook for 8 to 10 hours (sometimes I put this on to cook late at night and let it cook all night).
Add potatoes, carrot and onions for last hour of so of cooking.

Oven Method:

Set oven at 350 degrees.
Line a roasting pan with aluminum foil (easy clean up).
Place pot roast in bottom of pan.
Pour both cans of soup over the pot roast.
Pour two cans of water over the pot roast.
Cover with aluminum foil.
Bake for about 3 hours or until tender.
Place potatoes, carrots and onions on top of pot roast for the last hour of baking.

Note: Sometimes, if the crockpot is large enough, I do two pot roasts at once for larger crowds. Either way this pot roast is fork tender, great flavor and couldn't be any easier!

Fruited Pot Roast
Margaret Wroth Johansen

4 lbs. arm roast
12 whole apricots
12 whole prunes
1-1/2 cups onions, sliced
1 cup apple juice
2 tablespoons sugar
¼ teaspoon cinnamon
¼ teaspoon ginger
3 whole cloves
1 teaspoon Worcestershire sauce
Salt and pepper
¼ cup flour

Cover apricots and prunes with water and soak for several hours.
Brown roast in dry hot pot.
Season with salt and pepper.
Top with sliced onions.
Combine apple juice, sugar, cinnamon, ginger and cloves.
Pour ½ of mixture over meat.
Cover and simmer 1 hour.
Then add balance of mixture and cook 1-1/2 hours.
Drain fruits and place on roast the last ½ hour.
Remove roast from pot to warm serving dish.

Add Worcestershire sauce to gravy.
Add enough water to make 1-1/2 cups of juice.
Make paste for gravy using ¼ cup of flour and enough water to make a paste.

Stir slowly into juice and cook to make gravy, stirring often.

Ristoff's Barbecue Ribs
Dot & Ted Ristoff

2 racks pork back ribs
1 liter Coke

Put ribs in a throw away aluminum pan.
Pour Coke over ribs.
Cover with foil.

Bake in 325-degree oven for 4 hours.
DO NOT check on the ribs until the 4 hours are up.

Remove ribs from pan and place them in another pan.
Discard cooking juice.

Brush heavily with barbecue sauce.
Brown either on a grill or oven broiler.

Serves 4

Author's Note: This recipe comes from Dot and Ted Ristoff in Troy, Ohio. They have been wonderful friends since the early '70s. I never really liked ribs until I started making them using this recipe!!

Salmon Patties
Hans Johansen, Jr.

2 slices bread, broken into small pieces
½ teaspoon dry mustard
1 can salmon, drained
¼ teaspoon salt
1 whole egg
1 teaspoon Worcestershire sauce
2 tablespoons vinegar

Mix all ingredients.
Shape into patties.
Fry in 2 tablespoons vegetable oil until brown on both sides.
4-5 minutes each side.

Favorite Spaghetti Sauce
Sheila Pitzer

1 lb. ground beef
¾ cup chopped onions
2 cloves garlic, crushed
3 16-ounce cans tomato sauce
1 16-ounce can stewed tomatoes
2 teaspoons dried oregano
2 teaspoons dried basil leaves
¼ teaspoon pepper
¼ teaspoon salt
1 tablespoon sugar

Brown ground beef in a skillet with onions and garlic.
Drain off excess fat.
Add remaining ingredients.
Heat to boiling.
Reduce heat.
Simmer gently for approximately 30 minutes.
Serve over hot spaghetti pasta.
Makes 7-1/2 cups

For meatless sauce, just omit the meat and simmer onions and garlic in 1 tablespoon oil and proceed same as above.

Note: This recipe was given to me from my friend, Mel Fields, several years ago for another event we were doing at church. It is a simple recipe but very good!

Patricia's Spaghetti
Alice Ogez Litzy Perkins

1 lb. hamburger
1 small onion
1 can 29 oz. (or 2, 15 oz. cans) Red Gold tomato sauce
1 15 oz. can Red Gold diced tomatoes
1/8 teaspoon garlic salt
1/8 teaspoon black pepper
1 small can mushrooms, drained
1 seasoning packet from Kraft Spaghetti Classics Tangy Italian meal kit
Spaghetti noodles
¼ stick Blue Bonnet margarine.

Brown and crumble ground beef.
Add diced onions and stick of butter; cook until onions are opaque.
In sauce pan, cook mushrooms with ¼ stick butter. Cook until mushrooms are browned.
Add mushrooms to hamburger mixture.
Add tomato sauce.
Warm mixture. Once warm, stir in seasoning packet and ensure no seasoning lumps remain.
Add diced tomatoes, garlic salt and pepper.
Cook for 25 minutes.
Add a small amount of water if sauce is too thick.
Serve over cooked spaghetti noodles, cooked tortellini, ravioli, etc.…
You can use the noodles out of the kit, but you will most likely need more noodles.

Note: Alice has recreated her Mother Patricia's spaghetti recipe from memory since her Mom never wrote down any recipes.

Spaghetti Sauce with Meat
Helen Salyer Perkins Johansen

1 lb. ground chuck
1 medium onion, finely chopped
1 small can sliced mushrooms, drained
1 package dry spaghetti sauce mix
1 28-ounce jar spaghetti sauce (Prego, Ragu, etc.)
1 28-ounce jar water
1 tablespoon cooking oil or olive oil
Parmesan or shredded cheddar cheese

Sauté onions in a heavy cooking pot in cooking oil or olive oil until they begin to brown.
Add ground chuck and cook until no longer red and beginning to brown.
Add mushrooms and cook over medium heat for 5 minutes.
Add dry spaghetti sauce mix and stir well.
Add liquid spaghetti sauce.
Fill spaghetti sauce jar with water, add lid and shake to loosen sauce left in jar.
Add water to mixture.

Bring to a boil, then cook on low heat for 1-2 hours or all afternoon if you want.

Serve over spaghetti pasta and top with Parmesan or shredded cheddar cheese.

Add a tossed salad and some crusty bread and you've got a great dinner!

Italian Style Meat Ball Spaghetti

Fern Storer
Cincinnati Post & Times-Star
January 18, 1967

1 lb. lean ground beef
1-1/2 cups small torn bread pieces (about two slices)
¼ cup grated Parmesan cheese
1 egg
2 tablespoons chopped parsley
1-1/2 teaspoons salt
½ teaspoon dried leaf basil
½ teaspoon dried leaf oregano
½ cup tomato juice (drained from tomatoes, below)
3 tablespoons shortening (part oil or vegetable shortening and part butter or margarine)

Sauce:

Shortening (left in skillet from above)
1 cup sliced celery
1 cup sliced onion
1 clove garlic, minced
½ teaspoon salt
½ teaspoon basil
1 can (28 ounces) tomatoes (minus ½ cup juice used above)
1 can (6 ounces) tomato paste
½ teaspoon sugar
¼ teaspoon pepper
1 bay leaf
1 package (7 or 8 ounces) spaghetti
¾ cup grated Parmesan cheese

In large mixing bowl combine the beef, bread, ¼ cup of cheese, egg, parsley, 1-1/2 teaspoons salt, basil, oregano and ½ cup liquid drained from tomatoes.
Mix well using a sturdy fork.

Italian Style Meat Ball Spaghetti (cont'd)

Shape meat mixture into balls about an inch and a quarter in diameter.

I like to shape all the meat balls and place them on waxed paper before starting the sautéing.

Heat shortening in large skillet on medium heat.
Sauté the meat balls (number you can do without crowding) in the fat, turning to brown on all sides. You needn't cook them completely.
Removed browned meat balls from skillet and continue with rest of them.
Set all the meat balls aside.

In fat remaining in skillet, sauté celery and onion on medium heat until just beginning to soften.
Scrape a place free on skillet bottom and add the finely minced garlic – cook only a few seconds.
Mix into rest of vegetables.
Add the ½ teaspoon salt, basil, tomatoes, tomato paste, sugar, pepper and bay leaf.
Cover pan and simmer sauce slowly for an hour to an hour and a half, stirring occasionally with your straight-end stirrer.
The long, gentle cooking mellows the flavors.

Now add the meat balls, gently pressing them down into the sauce.
Cover and simmer gently for 45 minutes to an hour.

Cook spaghetti as directed on package.
Drain and serve topped with the meat balls and spaghetti sauce.
Sprinkle with grated Parmesan cheese.

This meat balls sauce may be prepared a day or two ahead and refrigerated.

Italian Style Meat Ball Spaghetti (cont'd)

Gently reheat (in covered skillet or saucepan) the amount you will need for a meal and serve over hot freshly cooked spaghetti.

This is a good way to do most of the work for a couple of good meals on the weekend.
Then all you have to do is cook the spaghetti and reheat the sauce when you come home from a busy day.

Variation on Sauce:

Rich Italian Spaghetti Sauce

¼ cup olive oil (or at least half olive oil and half other cooking oil)
4 medium-sized onions, chopped
2 tablespoons finely minced parsley
4 cloves garlic, finely minced
2 8-ounce cans tomato soup
2 6-ounce cans tomato paste
½ teaspoon salt
2 teaspoons Worcestershire sauce
1 lb. lean ground beef
Grated Parmesan cheese

In medium heavy saucepan, heat shortening and in it, sauté the onions and parsley until onions are slightly soft.
Scrape a place free on pan bottom and drop the minced garlic on this; sauté only a few seconds then stir into onion mixture.
Add tomato soup and tomato paste; rinse the cans with a little water and add.
Add salt and Worcestershire sauce.
Let sauce simmer gently while you brown the meat in a medium-sized skillet.

Do not cook the meat too long; it should not get hard and crusty; just cook until red color is out.
Add meat to sauce and cook slowly for about three hours.

Serve over hot cooked spaghetti.
Sprinkle grated Parmesan over top.

Spicy Tuna Roll
Jessica Green Ward

3 raw tuna steaks
3 tablespoons Miracle Whip
1 tablespoon chili powder (or desired spiciness)
Several sheets of Nori (seaweed)
3 cups sticky rice
Sesame seeds
Bamboo mat

With hands, smash tuna steaks.
Add Miracle Whip and chili powder.
Prepare sticky rice according to package instructions and let cool.
On one side of Nori, apply sticky rice in thin layer.
Sprinkle with sesame seeds.
Flip over and add a strip of tuna mixture down one edge of Nori.
Place on bamboo mat and roll tight.
Cut with Sushi knife and chill.

Makes about 6 to 7 Sushi rolls.

Baking a Turkey
Helen Salyer Perkins Johansen

- ½ to ¾ lbs. of turkey per person to be served.

- Fresh – pick up on Tuesday or Wednesday before Thanksgiving and keep in refrigerator.

- Frozen – move from freezer to refrigerator on Monday afternoon to thaw – do NOT thaw on counter.

- Turkey breast works very well if no one likes dark meat.

- Unwrap, free legs and tail, then remove giblets and neck piece from cavities.

- Thoroughly rinse bird and pat dry.

- Don't stuff bird until you're ready to bake it.

- To stuff – spoon stuffing loosely into neck cavity. Pull neck skin over stuffing and fasten to back with skewer. Place bird, neck side down, in large bowl. Loosely spoon stuffing into body cavity. Do not pack. Tuck drumsticks under band of skin across tail or tie legs to tail. Twist wing tips under back of bird.

- A cooking bag can be used; just follow the directions on the box.

- Cooking time – 20-25 minutes per pound in open roasting pan at 325 degrees. See directions on turkey packaging.

For open roasting, place turkey, breast side up, on rack in shallow pan. Brush with cooking oil. If you use a meat

Baking a Turkey (cont'd)

- thermometer, put it into the center of inside thigh muscle so bulb doesn't touch bone.

- Cover bird loosely with foil, leaving space between bird and foil. Press foil lightly at end of drumsticks and neck. Baste occasionally with butter, margarine or drippings. When bird is 2/3 done, cut skin or string on legs. Remove foil for the last 30-45 minutes to brown.

- If using a covered roasting pan, add just a small amount of water. Roast with vent open.

- Remove stuffing from turkey immediately after the meal and place in a separate container for storing.

Note: See recipe for Bread Dressing/Stuffing under the Casserole section.

Herb Baked Turkey
Dana Graham Perkins

13 lb. turkey
Onions, quartered
Sprigs of fresh rosemary
Salt and pepper

Stuff the cavity of the turkey with the onions, salt and pepper and a couple sprigs of fresh rosemary.

In a bowl, combine:
¾ cup of olive oil
2 tablespoons garlic powder
2 teaspoons dried basil
1 teaspoon dried sage
1 teaspoon salt
½ teaspoon black pepper
Softened butter

Use this mixture to massage the underside and then the outside of the bird.

Take some fresh rosemary or basil or whatever you have and squish together with some softened butter. Run your hand under the skin of the bird all the way down the front and rub the butter on the breast, etc. Be careful not to puncture the skin. Rub the butter all under the skin wherever you can.

Layer the bottom of your roasting pan with fresh vegetables – carrots, onions and celery – making a vegetable rack instead of using a metal rack in the bottom. Put some water in the bottom of the pan and cook according to directions on the wrapper of the bird.

Discard the cavity vegetables and the vegetables on the bottom of the pan after cooking.   Let bird rest 30 minutes before carving.

Turkey Pot Pie
Helen Salyer Perkins Johansen

After everyone has had their fill of leftovers, line a buttered 9x13 baking dish with pie dough.

Layer turkey, dressing, mashed potatoes, leftover vegetables and/or frozen mixed vegetables in dish.

Cover with leftover gravy, cream of chicken or cream of celery soup.

Place strips of pie dough lengthwise and widthwise or just one sheet of pie dough over top of the leftovers.

Bake at 325 degrees for 30 to 40 minutes or until crust is brown. Serve with leftover cranberry sauce or salad.

This is a delicious way to use up your leftovers from Thanksgiving dinner!

Wing Sauce

Greg & Kim Evans
Crossroads Family Restaurant & Gift Shop
615 West Highway 50
Versailles, IN 47042

1 cup Franks Cayenne Pepper sauce
1/3 cup vegetable oil
1 teaspoon sugar
½ teaspoon cayenne pepper
½ teaspoon garlic powder
1 teaspoon Worcestershire sauce
¼ teaspoon black pepper
1 egg yolk
2 tablespoons water
1 tablespoon corn starch

Combine all ingredients and heat until boiling.

Remove from heat and let cool.

Combine egg yolk, water and corn starch.

Mix well and add to warm mixture.

Notes:

NOODLES & DUMPLINGS

Apple Dumplings
Evalyn Clutters (Mrs. Tom) Tolliver

2 cups flour
1 teaspoon salt
1 cup Crisco
6 tablespoons water
6 apples, peeled and cored
Sugar, cinnamon and nutmeg

Mix flour, salt, Crisco and water to make dough.
Divide dough into six (6) parts.
Roll each out.
Place an apple on each part, and sprinkle with sugar, cinnamon and nutmeg.
Fold dough up and over the apple.
Place dumplings in baking dish.

Syrup:

2 cups boiling water
1 stick butter
1-1/2 cups sugar

Bring to boil and pour syrup over dumplings.
Sprinkle with nutmeg on top.

Bake in 400-degree oven for 1 hour.

Baked Noodles
Priscilla Pyles Huff

1 cup cottage cheese
1 cup sour cream
½ cup onions, chopped
1 teaspoon Worcestershire Sauce
½ teaspoon garlic salt
6-ounce package fine egg noodles, cooked
12 crackers, crushed
Melted butter

Mix first five ingredients.

Add cooked noodles and mix.

Pour in buttered baked dish or 8x8 pan.

Mix crushed crackers and butter.

Sprinkle over noodle mixture.

Bake at 350-degrees for 35 minutes.

Cherry Dumplings
Edna Tolliver Hayes Hollandsworth

1 pint bag frozen cherries
1 cup sugar or more to taste
1-1/2 cups water
1/8 teaspoon salt
¼ - ½ teaspoons red food coloring
2 tablespoons cornstarch
1/3 cup water

Combine first five ingredients in a large pan with a lid.
Bring to a boil.
Have ready 2 tablespoons cornstarch mixed with 1/3 cup water.
When cherry mixture is boiling hot, stir cornstarch mixture till well mixed.
Pour cornstarch mixture quickly into cherries all at once, stirring so it won't lump.
If you pour it in without stirring rapidly, the cornstarch will cook in a lump and spoil the juice.
Taste the juice and if not sweet enough, add more sugar.
If too thick, add more hot water, a small amount at a time until juice is syrupy but not too thick.

Cut a can of 10 biscuits in two pieces each.
Lay on top of hot cherry mixture.

Cover and reduce heat to very low for 10 to 12 minutes.
Don't lift the pot lid while cooking slow.

Serve with a scoop of ice cream while warm.

Other canned or fresh fruits can be used rather than cherries.

Homemade Chicken or Beef Noodles
Edna Tolliver Hayes Hollandsworth

Bony pieces of chicken or stew beef
Salt
Pepper, if desired

2 eggs
½ teaspoon salt
Yellow food coloring
Flour

Cook chicken pieces or stew beef to make broth.
Bone chicken carefully after cooking very tender in water, salt and pepper.
Make about 1 quart or more of broth.

Combine eggs, salt and a little yellow food coloring.
Add enough flour to make a very stiff dough.
Turn dough out on a floured surface.
Knead until smooth, using plenty of flour.

Roll out to paper thin, using plenty of flour so dough won't stick together.
Cut in 1-1/2 inch strips with a very sharp knife.
Stack the strips.
Cut into two shorter stacks and stack together.
Cut in very thin slices on cutting board.
So edges won't stick together as you cut, add flour plentifully.

Add noodles to boiling broth a few at a time, stirring to keep them separated.
Reduce heat and cook slowly till done.
The flour will form gravy.

Homemade Noodles
Ruby Tolliver Brewster

3 egg yolks or 1 whole egg
1 tablespoon evaporated milk (or regular milk)
Yellow food coloring
1 teaspoon salt
Flour
Chicken or beef broth

Add egg, milk and salt to taste.
Add a drop of yellow food coloring to the noodle dough and the broth.
Add enough flour to make a very stiff dough.
Roll out on floured counter until very thin.
Cut into about 2-1/2-inch strips.
Sprinkle flour in between and stack strips.
Cut in half and stack again.
Cut thin strips through whole stack.

Sprinkle into broth, stirring constantly to keep noodles from sticking together.
Put on simmer and cover.

Cook 20 to 30 minutes.

Too much broth, add thickening.
Too many noodles, add water.

Chicken pieces can be added if desired.

Noodles
Mary Smith (Mrs. Ulis) Tolliver

1 cup flour
1 egg
2 tablespoons evaporated milk
½ teaspoon salt

Mix egg, milk and salt to taste.
Add enough flour to make a very stiff dough.
Roll out thin.

Cut into 2-1/2-inch strips.
Sprinkle flour in between and stack strips.
Cut in half and stack again.
Cut thin strips through whole stack.

Sprinkle noodles into boiling chicken or beef broth, stirring constantly.
Put on simmer and cover.

Cook 20 to 30 minutes.

Too much broth, add thickening.
To many noodles, add water.

Author's Note: Many of the Tolliver girls or daughters-in-law made noodles but each had their special way of making them. Anyone tasting noodles at the family reunion could most likely identify who made them just by the look and taste of the dish.

Noodles and Tomatoes
Pearl Tolliver Simpson

Noodles:
3 eggs
Salt and pepper
Flour

Beat eggs, season with salt and pepper.
Add flour to make very stiff dough.
Knead on floured board.
Roll very thin.
Cut into strips, stack strips and cut crosswise into noodles.

Tomatoes
Butter
Salt and Pepper

Boil tomatoes.
Season with butter and salt and pepper.
Drop noodles into boiling tomatoes, a few at a time.

Mom's Noodles and Dumplings
Helen Salyer Perkins Johansen

Noodles

1 egg, beaten
½ teaspoon salt
Flour

Mix egg, salt and add flour until stiff.
Knead on counter or board until solid.
Let dough rest for a while.
Roll out into thin sheet – about ¼ inch.
Cut into 1-1/2 inch strips.
Stack strips on top of each other, several at a time.
Cut into strips as narrow or wide as you like.
Spread noodles out on the counter or board where you rolled out the dough.
Allow noodles to dry for several hours or overnight.

Add a few noodles at a time to boiling chicken or beef broth with or without meat.
Cover and simmer until noodles are tender.
Flour that is still on the noodles will allow broth to thicken.
If broth is too thick, add a bit of warm water or broth.

Dumplings

2 cups flour
½ teaspoon salt
¼ teaspoon baking soda
1 teaspoon baking powder
2 tablespoons Crisco
Yellow food coloring
Buttermilk

Mom's Noodles and Dumplings (cont'd)

Sift together flour, salt, soda and baking powder.
Add Crisco and cut into flour mixture with a fork.
Add enough buttermilk to make a stiff dough.
Add a drop or two of yellow food coloring, if desired.

Bring a large pot of chicken or beef broth to a boil.
Drop dumplings by the spoonful into the boiling broth.
Dumplings will rise to the top quickly.
Gently nudge the ones on the top over to make room for additional dumplings.

When all are added, simmer with a lid on the pot for about 10-15 minutes.

DO NOT STIR!

The Pink Noodle Story

Aunt Ruby's daughter Teresa sent me the following "noodle" story. Just had to add it.

As you know, Mom made the best noodles ever. Sometimes she'd make chicken and noodles, and sometimes she'd make beef and noodles. My favorite was beef. She made them every year for the Tolliver family reunion. She would mix up the noodles, roll the dough out into thin layers, stack the layers, then cut them into thin strips with one of the old fashioned knives that she found at a yard sale somewhere and sharpened on a whetstone. Man were those knives sharp. When the noodles were done, she would wrap the entire pot, right off the stove, in newspapers. Then she'd wrap a dish towel around the newspaper and hold it all together with sewing pins. This was to keep the noodles hot until we drove "down in the hills" to Grandma Tolliver's house. I think every single year of my life up until Mom passed, I saw her go through this routine.

So, the Tolliver reunion was coming up, and of course Mom was going to make noodles. Aunt Bertha came to my house to spend the night. Mom was spending the night, too. Then we were all going to ride to the reunion together. The night before the reunion, Mom proceeded to make her famous chicken and noodles. When she got the dough mixed up, there was one very important task that was her secret to making good homemade noodles. FOOD COLOR. She wanted to make her noodles look "eggy", so she always added a few drops of orange food coloring to the dough. Everyone raved and raved about how good her noodles looked, and she used to chuckle about the food coloring secret.

Unfortunately, the night before the reunion when she got the dough mixed up at my house, we discovered that I had NO orange food coloring. Oh, what a dilemma. It was too late to go to the store. Of course, Mom said, "Dear, oh me! What am I gonna do

The Pink Noodle Story (cont'd)

without orange food coloring? The noodles won't be a bit good without it." Aunt Bertha tried to console her and assured her that the noodles would be great without it, but Mom wasn't having it. I had the basic food colors, just not the orange. Being the amateur artist that I am, I suggested that we mix red and yellow food coloring to make orange. Mom was skeptical but didn't have a lot of options, so she agreed.

She and I and Aunt Bertha all diligently talked amongst ourselves as to how much of each color we should add. She was making a lot of noodles, so there was lots of dough. A couple drops of yellow. A few drops of red. Mom stirred and stirred with high hopes. The more she stirred, the more horrified we all became. The noodles were NOT turning dark yellow like they normally did. They turned PINK! Mom stirred more furiously, and we added another drop or two here and there. But no matter what we did, the noodles just got pinker and pinker. When we all realized that there was nothing, we could do to fix it, Aunt Bertha started quietly giggling. She made me laugh, and when Mom looked up at both of us, she laughed and laughed with us. After we'd all had a good laugh, Mom finished the noodles.

She threw them in to cook the next morning. Throughout the entire process of getting ready for the reunion, each of us made little jokes about the pink noodles. Mom said maybe nobody would notice, and Aunt Bertha said, "Well no, no one would notice!" The noodles were excellent. No one mentioned the noodle color and, like they normally would, all of them were eaten by the end of the day. I don't know if anyone noticed or if everyone was just too polite to say anything about it. I'm pretty sure they would have mentioned it though since it was a Tolliver reunion, and as you know, the Tolliver's aren't much to mince words. We are all pretty blunt. Which I love.

The Pink Noodle Story (cont'd)

For many years after that, the pink noodles would come up in conversation between us, and we would have a good laugh over what happened to the noodles that reunion. Boy, do I miss those noodles. And boy, do I miss her laugh!

Notes:

OTHER DESSERTS

Karen Pence's Famous Next Best Thing to Tom Selleck

Second Lady Karen Pence

1 stick butter or margarine
1 cup flour
2 tablespoons sugar
¼ cup chopped pecans
8 ounces cream cheese
8 ounces Cool Whip
1 cup confectioners' sugar
1 small package vanilla pudding & pie filling
1 small package chocolate pudding & pie filling
3 cups milk

First Layer:

Melt butter over low heat
Stir in flour, sugar and pecans.
Press onto bottom of a 9x13 baking dish.
Bake in 350-degree oven for 15 minutes.
Cool.

Second Layer:

Beat together until smooth: cream cheese (at room temperature), half of the Cool Whip and confectioner's sugar.
Spread over the cooled crust and refrigerate.

Third Layer:

Combine both packages of pudding with the 3 cups of milk.
Cook over medium heat, stirring constantly until mixture begins to thicken.

Karen Pence's Famous Next Best Thing to Tom Selleck (cont'd)

Cool and spread over the cream cheese mixture.
Chill thoroughly.

Fourth Layer:

Spread the remaining Cool Whip over the chocolate mixture.
Sprinkle with chopped nuts.

Author's Note: In the late 1990's and early 2000's, I hosted Kitchen Korner which was a radio cooking program on WNVI radio in North Vernon, Indiana. Now Vice President Mike Pence was a guest on my program and brought this recipe with him. He was a delightful guest and although he stated he didn't cook, he was well acquainted with the outcome of this recipe. One of his comments was that if you plan to make it to take to a dinner, it's best to make two of them, since if there is only one in the refrigerate, it will disappear before you are able to get it to the dinner!

Apricot or Prune Whip
Hans Johansen, Jr.

1-1/2 cups sweetened apricot or prune pulp
1-1/2 tablespoons lemon juice
1/8 teaspoon salt
1/3 cup sugar
3 egg whites, stiffly beaten
Chopped nuts

Combine pulp, lemon juice and salt.
Beat sugar into stiffly beaten egg whites.

Fold pulp mixture into egg whites.

Serve garnished with chopped nuts.

If desired, this mixture can be piled lightly into a buttered baking dish and baked at 275 degrees for 30 to 45 minutes.

Baklava
Kathy Lafakis

Ingredients:

1 lb. walnuts
½ lb. almonds
1 lb. filo dough, thawed
1/3 cup sugar
2 teaspoons vanilla
2 teaspoons cinnamon
1 lb. unsalted butter melted

Grind walnuts and almonds very fine in large bowl.
Add sugar, vanilla and cinnamon.
Mix well and set aside.

Assembly:

Brush 9x13 pan with melted butter.
Place one filo sheet in the buttered pan then brush that sheet with butter – continue filo-butter-filo-butter… for 7 sheets of filo.
Place the 8th sheet but do not brush the 8th filo sheet with butter.
Sprinkle it with 1/3 of the nut mixture on the 8th sheet

Then the filo layers again filo-butter-filo… for 7 filo sheets
Do not brush the 8th filo sheet. Sprinkle 1/3 of the nut mixture on the 8th sheet

Repeat for 7 more sheets of the remaining filo for the top of baklava (butter these liberally).

Place the pan of baklava in the freezer for about 15 minutes to make it easy to cut.

Remove from freezer.

Baklava (cont'd)

Using a sharp knife, cut into 1 inch diamond-shaped pieces.

Bake in preheated oven for 50-60 minutes or until medium brown in color.

While the Baklava is in the oven prepare the syrup:

1 cup of water
2 cups of sugar
½ cup of honey
1 teaspoon lemon juice

Mix all ingredients together.
Cook over medium heat until they come to a boil.
Reduce heat to low and cook 15-20 minutes.
Cool syrup slightly.
Pour syrup evenly over baklava.

Cover with wax paper. Let sit at room temperature for about 4 hours before cutting and serving.

Note from Jimmy Lafakis, Kathy's son: Baklava is probably the best known Greek pastry. It is one of my Mom's favorite desserts to make because the recipe was given to her by her grandmother. She entered this recipe in a Baklava Contest at a nearby Greek Festival and won 2nd place out of 24 entries. I hope you enjoy this recipe as much as our family does.

Banana Split Lasagna

Mary Etta Roth
Grateful Grubb Family Restaurant
412 South Madison Avenue
North Vernon, IN 47265
812-346-0004

2 cups graham cracker crumbs
½ cup (1 stick) butter, melted
1 8-ounce package cream cheese, softened
½ teaspoon vanilla
¼ cup sugar
2 tablespoons plus 3-1/2 cups milk, divided
1 16-ounce container Cool Whip
1 23-ounce bag frozen sliced strawberries, thawed and well drained
1 20-ounce can crushed pineapple, well drained
2 small boxes instant banana pudding mix
Chocolate syrup

In a medium bowl, combine graham cracker crumbs and melted butter.
Stir the mixture until it is evenly moist.
Pour crumb mixture into a 9x13 baking dish and press into an even layer.
Set in refrigerator while preparing next layer.

In medium bowl, combine cream cheese, sugar, 2 tablespoons of milk and vanilla with mixer on medium speed.
Mix together until fluffy and light.
Mix in 8-ounce Cool Whip.

Once completely combined, remove your baking dish from the fridge and spread the cream cheese mixture on top of the graham cracker crust.

Banana Split Lasagna (cont'd)

Spoon drained strawberries and pineapple on top of the cream cheese mixture and spread it evenly. It doesn't matter which fruit you use first.
Mix puddings with 3-1/2 cups cold milk.
Whisk for a few minutes until the pudding starts to thicken.
Spread the pudding over the fruit layer.

Let the dessert sit for about 5 minutes so that the pudding can firm up a bit.

Spread 8-ounce Cool Whip over the top.

Drizzle chocolate syrup on top of Cool Whip.

Chill at least 4 hours or overnight.

Blueberry Angel Dessert
Jayme Hartwell

Preparation time: 10 minutes + chilling

Ingredients:

1 package (8 ounces) cream cheese, softened
1 cup confectioner's sugar
1 carton (8 ounces) frozen whipped topping, thawed
1 prepared angel food cake (8 to 10 ounces), cut into 1-inch cubes
2 cans (21 ounces each) blueberry pie filling

Directions:

In a large bowl, beat cream cheese and confectioner's sugar until smooth.
Fold in whipped topping and cake cubes.
Spread evenly into an ungreased 13 x 9 inch dish.
Top with pie filling.
Refrigerate, covered, at least 2 hours before serving.

Yield: 12 servings.

Blueberry Angel Food Cake
kimbensen.com

1 box sugar-free blueberry gelatin
¾ cup boiling water
½ cup cold water
1 prepackaged sugar-free angel food cake
1-1/2 cups cold nonfat milk
1 box vanilla fat-free, sugar-free pudding mix
1 teaspoon vanilla extract, optional
8-ounce container fat-free whipped topping
1 cup blueberries
1 tablespoon sliced almonds

In a small bowl, dissolve gelatin in boiling water.
Stir in the cold water and set aside.
Cut the cake into 2" slices and arrange in a 9x13 baking dish.
With a meat fork or similar utensil, poke holes in the cake about 2" apart.
Slowly pour the blueberry gelatin over the cake.
Refrigerate for 1-2 hours or until gelatin is set.

In a bowl, whisk the milk and pudding mix for 2 minutes.
Whisk in the vanilla extract, if desired.
Let stand for 2 minutes or until soft-set.
Fold in the whipped topping.
Spread over the cake.
Garnish with blueberries and almonds.
Cover and refrigerate for 1 hour prior to serving.

Note: Fresh strawberries and strawberry gelatin can be substituted for the blueberry gelatin and blueberries.

Gerri's Wildcat Blueberry Cream Puff
Geraldine Green Miracle

1 cup flour
1 cup water
½ cup margarine
4 eggs

Heat oven to 400 degrees.

Boil water and margarine in 1-quart saucepan.
Stir in flour and beat vigorously until ball forms.
Remove from heat.
Place in mixer bowl and add eggs.
Beat until smooth.
Drop by tablespoon onto greased pan to form design of choice.
Smooth with spatula.

Bake until puffed and golden brown – 50-60 minutes.
Cool pastry.
Cut off top with sharp knife.
Pull out and discard soft dough in center.

Filling:

1-1/2 cups sour cream
2 packages vanilla *instant* pudding (3-1/2 oz each)
½ teaspoon almond extract
2 cups milk
1-2 cans blueberry pie filling (I use two)
Fresh blueberries for garnish

Add milk, sour cream, dry pudding mix and almond extract in mixing bowl.
Beat with mixer until well blended.
Fill pastry with pudding mixture.

Gerri's Wildcat Blueberry Cream Puff (cont'd)

Spoon one (1) can blueberry pie filling on top of pudding mixture. Replace top and add remaining can of pie filling on top of pastry. Garnish with fresh blueberries.
Refrigerate until serving time.

Author's Note: Gerri made this Wildcat Blueberry Cream Puff on the Rachael Ray Show a few years ago. The name comes as no surprise since she is a graduate and avid fan of the University of Kentucky Wildcats!

Variations:

Any *instant* pudding or flavor of pie filling can be used.

Use cherry pie filling and make the puff in the shape of a wreath for Christmas. Garnish with holly or in the shape of a heart for Valentine's Day.

Using Chocolate Regal Sauce instead of pie filling makes a wonderful Éclair.

Chocolate Regal Sauce

½ cup corn syrup
1 cup sugar
1 cup water
3-ounce square unsweetened chocolate
1 teaspoon vanilla
1 cup Eagle Brand milk

Combine syrup, sugar and water. Cook to soft-ball stage. Remove from heat. Add chocolate square. Stir until chocolate melts. Add vanilla very slowly. Add Eagle Brand milk. Mix thoroughly. Cool. (Heat over hot water for a great hot fudge sauce.)

Cream Puffs
Ruby Tolliver Brewster

1 cup water
½ cup butter
1 cup flour
4 eggs

Heat water and butter to a rolling boil in a saucepan.
Stir in flour all at once.
Stir vigorously over low heat until mixture leaves sides and bottom of pan and forms a ball – about 1 minute.
Remove from heat.

Beat in eggs, one at a time.
Beat until smooth and velvety.

Drop from spoon onto ungreased baking sheet.

Bake at 400 degrees for 45-50 minutes until dry.

Makes 8 large puffs.

You can slice and fill with Thank You Pie Filling and whipped cream, if desired.

Mocha Berry Tortilla Cups
kimbensen.com

1 light flat bread or thin tortilla shells
Butter spray
1 teaspoon sugar
½ teaspoon ground cinnamon
1 cup nonfat milk
2 teaspoons instant coffee granules
1 box sugar-free, fat-free instant vanilla pudding mix
1 cup fat-free whipped topping
1-1/2 cups fresh berries, such as blueberries, raspberries and sliced strawberries

Cut flat bread into 4 equal sections.
Gently press each into a mini tostada pan; pleat edges.
Spray lightly with butter spray.
Combine sugar and cinnamon and sprinkle over tortillas.
Bake at 350 degrees for 8-10 minute or until crisp and lightly browned.
Cool on a wire rack.

In a small bowl, combine the milk and coffee granules until dissolved.
Add pudding mix and whisk for 2 minutes.
Let stand for 2 minutes or until soft-set.

Fold in the whipped topping.
Cover and refrigerate for 1 hour.

Remove from fridge, spoon ½ cup of the mixture into each baked tortilla cup.

Top with 1/3 cup of fresh berries.

Nutter Butter Dessert
Angela Huff Spurgeon

1 package Nutter Butter cookies
2 8-ounce tubs Cool Whip
1 8-ounce box cream cheese
2 cups powdered sugar
2 3-3/4 ounce boxes Butterscotch Instant Pudding

Crush cookies by hand (will be coarse) and pour almost all into a 9 x 13 baking dish.
Pat down for bottom layer.

In a big bowl, mix one tub of Cool Whip, cream cheese and powdered sugar thoroughly.
Gently spread over cookie crumb layer.

Prepare instant pudding as directed on box and spread over Cool Whip, cream cheese and powdered sugar mixture layer.

Spoon the remaining tub of Cool Whip on top and gently spread as top layer.

Sprinkle remaining cookie crumbs on top.

Chill for 30 minutes.

Store in refrigerator.

Easy Peach Cobbler
Helen Salyer Perkins Johansen

2 lb. frozen or fresh prepared peaches
1 box yellow cake mix
1 can diet lemon-lime soda

Spread frozen peaches in 9x13 pan sprayed with cooking spray.

Sprinkle dry cake mix over peaches.

Pour lemon-lime soda over cake mix.

Cover with foil and bake for 20 minutes at 350 degrees.

Uncover and bake for 40 minutes.

Enjoy!!

Raisin Molasses Bars

Edna Tolliver Hays Hollandsworth

4 cups white sugar
8 teaspoons baking soda
6 teaspoons cinnamon
3 teaspoons salt
12 cups flour
1 cup molasses
4 eggs
1 cup water
4 pounds raisins*
2-1/4 cups Crisco
1 ounce milk (to brush top of bars)

Mix all ingredients (except milk) well.
Divide into 12 balls.
Roll with hands on dough board to length of cookie sheet.
Should be about 1-1/4 inches in diameter.

Press down to about ½ inch thick.
Brush with milk.

Bake 20 minutes in 350-degree oven.
When cool, cut into bars 1-1/2 inches wide.

*Bars can be made with dates instead of raisins.

Author's Note: This recipe is similar to Willa's recipe for "Grandma's Stack Cake / Cookies" using water rather than buttermilk and cinnamon instead of ginger. Making the recipe into bars rather than a cake or cookies is an interesting twist which would result in a large amount of wonderful, rich-tasting treats.

Glazed Cinnamon Scones
Susan Wisecup – from Money Saving Mom

Scone Ingredients:
2 cups flour
2 teaspoons baking powder
½ teaspoon baking soda
½ teaspoon salt
½ cup butter
1 egg, separated
3 tablespoons honey
1/3 cup buttermilk

Crumb Topping:
1-2 tablespoon Turbinado sugar *
½ teaspoon cinnamon

Glaze Ingredients:
1 cup powdered sugar
1-3 teaspoons milk (enough to make a glaze)
½ teaspoon vanilla

Preheat oven to 400 degrees.
Combine flour, baking powder, baking soda and salt.
Cut in butter until mixture is crumbly.
Separate egg white and yolk. Set the egg white aside.
In a separate bowl, mix egg yolk, honey and buttermilk.
Add to the dry ingredients and stir until ***just combined***.
Form dough into a ball on a floured surface.
Roll or pat out to half an inch thickness and eight inches in diameter.
Cut into eight equally sized pieces.
Transfer to a greased baking sheet.

Glazed Cinnamon Scones (cont'd)

Whisk the egg white until froth forms and brush over the tops of the scones.
Mix the turbinado sugar and cinnamon together and sprinkle over egg white topped scones.

Bake at 400 degrees for 10 to 12 minutes.

Mix together powdered sugar, milk and vanilla until a glaze forms. Drizzle glaze over scones after they bake.

*   *Turbinado sugar is evaporated cane juice and is sweet, rich and creamy with a distinctive crunchy texture. Substitutes are Demerara sugar, raw sugar, maple sugar, evaporated cane juice, light brown sugar, dark brown sugar, sucanat, and cinnamon sugar. Turbinado sugar gets its name from the turbine that is used to spin freshly squeezed sugar cane and turn it into Turbinado sugar.*

Notes:

PIES

Banana Cream Pie
Edna Tolliver Hayes Hollandsworth

Fresh bananas
3-ounce package vanilla cream pudding and pie filling
Baked pie shell

Cook pudding and pie filling as directed on box.
Pour into baked pie shell.

Cover with Saran Wrap and chill.

When ready to serve, slice fresh bananas on each piece as you serve it.

Top with Cool Whip.

If you slice the bananas on the whole pie and cover it, the fruit will turn dark and get stale.

Serves 6 or more.

Linda's Easy Blackberry Cobbler
Linda Tolliver Richard

2 quarts blackberries
1-1/2 cups sugar
1 teaspoon lemon juice
3 tablespoons butter
2 store-bought pie shells

Line iron skillet with one pie shell.

Combine blackberries, sugar and lemon juice.

Pour over the pie shell in the skillet.
Dot with butter.

Put second shell on top and seal where you can.

Bake at 375 degrees till golden brown.

Butterfinger Pie

Mary Etta Roth
Grateful Grubb Family Restaurant
412 South Madison Avenue
North Vernon, IN 47265
812-346-0004

1 8-ounce package cream cheese, softened
½ cup peanut butter
2 teaspoons vanilla
1-1/2 cups powdered sugar
1 bag small Butterfinger bars, crushed (reserve 2 bars to sprinkle on top)
1 8-ounce container Cool Whip
1 chocolate wafer pie crust

Beat cream cheese and peanut butter in mixer until smooth.
Mix in vanilla.
Beat in powdered sugar until smooth.
Fold in crushed Butterfingers.
Fold in Cool Whip.

Spread into crust and sprinkle reserved Butterfingers (crushed) on top.

Refrigerate at least 4 hours before serving.

Butterscotch Pie
Versa Tolliver Smith

2-1/2 cups light brown sugar
2-1/2 cups milk
5 tablespoons flour
3 egg yolks
½ cup margarine
2-1/2 teaspoons vanilla
1 unbaked pie crust

Mix all ingredients (except margarine) until smooth.
Place into medium saucepan and heat until smooth, stirring constantly.

When mixture starts to thicken, add margarine and continue stirring until thick and smooth.

Pour into pie crust and let cool.

Meringue:

Beat 3 egg whites until stiff.
Add ¼ cup sugar.
Beat well until all sugar dissolves.

Spread over pie.

Put in 350-degree oven until brown.

Buttermilk Pie
Mary Elizabeth Smith McDaniel Spurlock

2 cups sugar
8 tablespoons butter or margarine, softened
3 large eggs, room temperature
3 tablespoons flour
1 cup buttermilk
1 teaspoon vanilla
1/8 teaspoon nutmeg

Cream sugar and butter together and whip until fluffy.

Add eggs, flour and buttermilk.
Mix until smooth.

Add vanilla and nutmeg.

Pour into frozen 9-inch pie shell.

Bake at 350 degrees for about 45 or 50 minutes.

Check for doneness by ticking a toothpick into center. If it comes out clean, the pie is finished.

Charleston Coconut Pie
Priscilla Pyles Huff

4 eggs, beaten
½ cup self-rising flour
1-1/3 cups sugar or Splenda
½ stick butter
2 cups milk
8 ounces coconut
1 teaspoon vanilla

(Makes its own crust)

Beat all ingredients together.

Pour into greased 10-inch pie plate.

Bake at 350 degrees for 45 minutes.

Refrigerate.

Do not bake over 45 minutes!

Cherry Pie
Susan Matthews Wisecup
Taken from an old cookbook called Pies Men Like

3-1/2 cups fresh sour red cherries, pitted
or 2 cans tart cherries packed in water, drained
1-1/4 cups sugar
¼ cup flour
1 tablespoon butter
Cinnamon
Pastry for a 2-crust pie

Combine cherries, sugar and flour in a bowl. Set aside.
Line a 9-inch pie pan using half of the pastry.
Roll out the remaining pastry for the top crust and cut several slits for the steam to escape.
Pour the fruit mixture into the pie shell.
Dot with butter and sprinkle with cinnamon.
Adjust top crust on pie.
Seal edges, trim and flute.
Or slice the top crust into strips and make a lattice top instead.

Bake in a hot oven (400 degrees) 50 to 60 minutes.

Sprinkle with turbinado sugar about 15 minutes before pie is done.

Note: This was the recipe my Mom, Rosemary Simpson Matthews, used. She was frequently asked to bring this pie to gatherings of family and friends. She always made a lattice top on this pie. It was as pretty as it was good!

Cherry Cream Pie
Nell Chambers (Mrs. Roy) Tolliver

1-1/3 cups Eagle Brand milk (15 ounce)
1/3 cup lemon juice
1 cup whipped cream or 8-ounce cream cheese
1 teaspoon vanilla
½ teaspoon almond extract

Combine lemon juice, vanilla, almond extract and whipped cream.
Add mixture to Eagle Brand milk.
Pour into crust and chill.

Crust could be a regular baked pie crust containing crushed almonds in the crust or slivered almonds on top of the crust, or it could be a Graham cracker crust.

Cherry Topping

1 can or bag cherries (fresh or frozen), drained
2/3 cups cherry juice
¼ cup sugar
1 tablespoon corn starch

Combine cherry juice, sugar and corn starch.

Cook at low heat until thick and clear, stirring constantly.

Add cherries and spread on cream filling.

Chill before serving.

Cherry Delight Pie
Priscilla Pyles Huff

1 8-ounce package of cream cheese, softened
½ cup sugar or Splenda
1 8-ounce container Cool Whip
1 can cherry pie filling
1 Graham cracker crust pie shell

Mix sugar and cream cheese.

Add Cool Whip and mix.

Pour into pie shell.

Top with cherry pie filling.

Chill at least 3 hours before serving.

Cherry Delight

Mary Etta Roth
Grateful Grubb Family Restaurant
412 South Madison Avenue
North Vernon, IN 47265
812-346-0004

1 8-ounce package cream cheese, softened
1 cup powdered sugar
1 8-ounce container Cool Whip
1 can cherry pie filling
Graham cracker pie crust

Mix cream cheese and powdered sugar with mixer until smooth.

Fold in Cool Whip.

Blend well and pour into graham cracker crust.

Spoon pie filling on top.

Chill for a few hours before serving.

Chess Pie
Willa Tolliver Salyer Lyons

3 cups sugar
1-1/2 tablespoons flour
¼ tablespoon salt
¾ cups margarine, melted
½ teaspoon vanilla
6 eggs, lightly beaten
½ cup milk, less 2 tablespoons
3 tablespoons meal
1-1/2 tablespoons lemon juice
1 cup chopped pecans
2 unbaked pie shells

Combine the margarine, sugar, flour, salt and vanilla.

Add eggs and mix well.

Stir in the meal, milk and lemon juice.

Mix well.

Add pecans and mix well.

Pour into unbaked pie shells.

Bake at 350 degrees for 50 minutes.

Chocolate Cream Pie
Geraldine Green Miracle

1/2 cup flour (do not level)
1 cup sugar
2 tablespoons cocoa
3 egg yolks (separate eggs and save whites for meringue)
2-1/2 cups milk
1 teaspoon vanilla

Note: Use serving spoons to measure; not measuring spoons.

Blend flour, sugar and cocoa together.
Add milk, a little at a time to make a paste.
Add rest of milk slowly as you stir over medium heat.

After mixture has begun to thicken, take part of the hot mixture out of the saucepan and stir in egg yolks.
Return the mixture with the egg yolks added to the original mixture in the saucepan.
Cook until thick.
Remove from heat.
Add vanilla.

Add chocolate mixture to pie crust (you can use Pillsbury's Rolled Refrigerated pie crust)
Add meringue to top. (See meringue recipe below)
Seal the meringue to the edge of the crust.
Put in oven and bake at 350 degrees until meringue is lightly browned.

If pie filling gets lumpy while cooking, stir vigorously with a wire whisk.

*Note: This recipe is as close as I can get after watching my Grandmother, Mary Salyer Wellman, make her delicious pie. Of course, she **never** used anything but a homemade pie crust!*

Chocolate Cream Pie (cont'd)

Meringue

3 egg whites
6 tablespoons sugar
¼ teaspoon cream of tartar
½ teaspoon vanilla

Heat oven to 350 degrees.

Beat egg whites with cream of tartar until frothy.
Gradually beat in sugar, a little at a time.
Continue beating until stiff and glossy and sugar is dissolved. Do not overbeat.
Beat in vanilla.

Pile meringue onto **hot** pie filling.
Carefully seal meringue to the edge of the crust to prevent shrinking and weeping.
Swirl up or pull up to points for a decorative top.

Bake 10-15 minutes or until delicately browned.

Cool away from drafts.

Coconut Pie
Sharon Ross Beck

1-1/4 cup sugar
1 stick margarine, melted
1 tablespoon flour
3 eggs, beaten
½ bag coconut (7 ounces)
¼ cup milk
1 teaspoon vanilla
2 unbaked pie shells

Combine all ingredients and pour into unbaked pie shell.

Bake at 350 degrees for 20 minutes.

May take a few minutes longer if filling is still "shaky".

Cottage Cheese Pie
Karen Funke White

Preheat oven to 350 degrees.

2 cups or a 16-ounce container small curd cottage cheese
1 cup sugar
½ teaspoon vanilla
1 egg
Pinch of salt
1 teaspoon milk
1 unbaked pie shell

Mix all above ingredients together.

Pour into unbaked pie shell.

Top with cinnamon and raisins.

Bake for one hour at 350 degrees or until knife comes out clean.

Refrigerate leftovers.

Note: This is an old German pie recipe that has been passed down for many years in the Funke family.

Custard Pie
Edna Tolliver Hayes Hollandsworth

2 cups milk, scalded
5 tablespoons sugar
¼ teaspoon nutmeg
3 eggs
1/8 teaspoon salt
½ teaspoon vanilla

Beat eggs slightly.
Add sugar, salt, nutmeg and vanilla.
Mix thoroughly.
Add hot milk **slowly** while stirring.
Pour into unbaked pastry lined pie pan.
Bake in hot oven – 425 degrees – until center is jelled; about 25 minutes.
Can reduce heat if it gets too brown before done in the center.

Serve plain or with whipped topping.

You can use a 9-inch pie crust, or you can make a thicker filling by using an 8-inch crust and fluting the crust high on edge of pan.

Serves 6 or more

Florida Pie
Norma Jones Dalton

1 can Eagle Brand milk
1 medium can crushed pineapple, drained
9 ounce container Cool Whip
1 large banana
1 cup chopped nuts
½ cup lemon juice.

Mix all ingredients together.

Place in two graham cracker crusts.

Chill 4-6 hours before serving.

German Chocolate Pie
From an Old Mennonite Cookbook

1-1/4 cups sugar
½ stick (4 tablespoons) margarine, melted
1 egg, beaten
1-1/2 tablespoons cocoa
2 tablespoons flour
1 small can evaporated milk
¾ cup nuts
9-inch unbaked pie shell

Mix all ingredients well.

Pour into unbaked pie shell.

Bake at 375 degrees for 30 to 35 minutes.

Impossible Pie
Hallie Vanosdol

1-1/2 cups sugar
½ cup self-rising flour
Pinch of salt
2 cups milk
4 tablespoons margarine, melted
1 teaspoon vanilla, if desired
1 cup shredded or flaked coconut
4 eggs
2 unbaked pie shells

Combine sugar, flour and salt.
Sift all together.

Beat eggs, milk, margarine and vanilla.
Add coconut and sifted ingredients.

Pour into pie shells.
Fills two 8-inch pie shells.

Bake at 350 degrees for 35 minutes.

This makes its own crust on top!

Fluffy Lemon Pie
Joan Neuenschwander Schug

1 package sugar-free instant vanilla pudding mix
1 teaspoon sugar-free lemonade mix (Crystal Light)
1 cup cold fat-free or 2% milk
1 carton (8 ounces) reduced fat or sugar-free Cool Whip
1 reduced fat graham cracker crust (8 inch)

Combine pudding mix and lemonade mix.
Whisk milk and pudding mixture for 2 minutes.

Let stand for 2 minutes – pudding will be stiff.

Fold in half of the Cool Whip and spread into crust.

Top with remaining Cool Whip.

Cover and chill for 2-3 hours or until set.

Note: You can substitute other instant pudding mixes and omit the lemonade mix, if desired.

Mom's Lemon Pie
Bonnie Salyer Vogel

4 egg yolks
1 cup sugar
2 tablespoons flour or 1 tablespoon cornstarch
1-1/4 cups milk
½ teaspoon lemon extract

Beat egg yolks and sugar.
Stir flour into milk until dissolved.
Stir flour mixture into eggs and sugar.

Cook over medium to low heat until it begins to boil and thicken, stirring often.
Add lemon extract.

Pour into baked pie crust.

Meringue

4 egg whites
¾ cup sugar
2 drops lemon extract

In mixing bowl, beat together until stiff peaks form.
Spread on filling and brown in 400 degree oven (10 minutes)

Note: Mom always made one for Dad and another for the rest of us. We all loved it. Olga Mae's version of lemon pie!

Old Fashioned Cream Pie
From an Old Mennonite Cookbook

½ cup white sugar
½ cup brown sugar
½ cup (scant) flour
½ teaspoon cinnamon
¼ teaspoon salt
1 pint heavy cream
9-inch unbaked pie shell

Mix first five (5) ingredients well.

Add 1 pint heavy cream.

Pour into 9-inch pie unbaked pie shell.

Bake at 450 degrees for 10 minutes.

Reduce oven temperature to 350 degrees and bake 40-50 minutes.

Never Fail Pie Meringue
Edna Tolliver Hayes Hollandsworth

1 tablespoon cornstarch
6 tablespoons white sugar
½ cup water
3 egg whites
dash of salt

Mix cornstarch, sugar, water and salt.
Cook together until thick and clear.
Beat egg whites until frothy.

Continue beating while pouring hot cooked mixture slowly into egg whites.
Continue beating until meringue stands in peaks.

Cover cooled pie filling in shell with meringue, sealing edges on crust.

Bake at 450 degrees until golden brown – about 5 to 7 minutes.

This makes enough for a very high topping for one pie or a thinner topping for two pies.

Crumb top crust for 1 pie

¼ cup brown sugar
¼ cup soft butter
½ cup flour

Mix together till crumbly and sprinkle over fruit pies. Best for apple!

Million Dollar Pie
Sis Caplinger

¼ cup lemon juice
1 can Eagle Brand milk
1 8-ounce carton Cool Whip
1 small can crushed pineapple, drained
1-1/2 cups coconut
1 cup chopped nuts
2 graham cracker crusts

Mix lemon juice, milk and Cool Whip.

Add crushed pineapple, coconut and nuts.

Mix well.

Pour equal amounts into each graham cracker crust.

Oatmeal Pie
Karen Tolliver Kratzer

¼ cup butter
½ cup sugar
2 eggs
½ teaspoon cinnamon
½ teaspoon cloves
¼ teaspoon salt
1 cup light corn syrup
1 cup old fashioned or quick oats
Chopped nuts, if desired.

Cream together butter and sugar til fluffy.

Beat in eggs, cinnamon, cloves and salt.

Stir in oats and syrup.

Add nuts, if desired.

Pour into unbaked pie shell.

Bake at 350 degrees for 45 minutes.

Peanut Butter Pie

Mary Etta Roth
Grateful Grubb Family Restaurant
412 South Madison Avenue
North Vernon, IN 47265
812-346-0004

8-ounce package cream cheese, softened
1 cup powdered sugar
1 cup peanut butter
8-ounce container Cool Whip
1 unbaked or graham cracker pie crust

Mix together the cream cheese and powdered sugar until smooth.

Add peanut butter and continue to mix.

Fold in Cool Whip.

Pour into crust and chill for a few hours.

Good Pie Crust
Edna Tolliver Hayes Hollandsworth

1 cup vegetable shortening, rounded
3 cups flour
Salt to taste
½ cup cold water

Mix ½ cup of the cold water and ½ cup of the flour and set aside.

Then mix the shortening and remaining flour and salt together till crumbly, being careful to get all the flour from the bottom of the bowl mixed in.
Then add the flour and water paste.
Mix with spoon until it can be handled.

Do not knead, just squeeze together and roll on floured board or clean brown paper bag.
About half of a grocery bag is great.
Inside of clean one can be reused if you scrape off bits of dough and flour and fold up till next time.

This can be made in double or triple batch and wrapped in wax paper in one crust amounts and frozen in freezer bags. Good as fresh!

Pie Pastry
KitchenAid Mixer Recipes

2-1/4 cups all-purpose flour   *(1 cup and 2 tablespoons)**
¾ teaspoons salt   *(3/8 teaspoon)*
½ cup shortening, well chilled   *(1/4 cup)*
2 tablespoons butter or margarine, well chilled   *(1 tablespoon)*
5 to 6 tablespoons cold water   *(2-1/2 to 3 tablespoons)*

Place flour and salt in mixer bowl.
Attach bowl and flat beater to mixer.
Turn to Stir Speed (very low) and mix about 15 seconds.
Cut shortening and butter into pieces and add to flour mixture.
Turn to Stir Speed and mix until shortening particles are size of small peas, 30-45 seconds.

Continuing on Stir Speed, add water, 1 tablespoon at a time, mixing until ingredients are moistened and dough begins to hold together.
Divide dough in half.
Pat each half into a smooth ball and flatten slightly.
Wrap in plastic wrap.
Chill in refrigerator 15 minutes.

Roll out half of dough to 1/8-inch thickness between sheets of waxed paper.
Fold pastry into quarters.
Ease into 8 or 9-inch pie plate and unfold, pressing firmly against bottom and sides.

For One-Crust Pie: Fold edge under. Crimp as desired. Add desired pie filling. Bake as directed.

For Two-Crust Pie: Trim pastry even with edge of pie plate. Using second half of dough, roll out another pastry crust. Add desired pie filling. Top with second pastry crust. Seal edge. Crimp as desired. Cut slits for steam to escape. Bake as directed.

Pie Pastry (cont'd)

For Baked Pastry Shell: Fold edge under. Crimp as desired. Prick sides and bottom with fork. Bake at 450 degrees for 8 to 10 minutes, or until lightly browned. Cool completely on wire rack and fill.

Alternate Method for Baked Pastry Shell: Fold edge under. Crimp as desired. Line shell with foil. Fill with pie weights or dried beans. Bake at 450 degrees for 10 to 12 minutes, or until edges are lightly browned. Remove pie weights and foil. Cool completely on wire rack and fill.

Yield: 8 servings (two 8 or 9-inch crusts)

Author's Note: I have made pie crusts for years – some good and some not so good! However, this recipe is excellent and yields a most flaky and delicious pie crust. For just one pie crust, use the ingredient quantities shown in italics. Practice makes perfect!!

Pumpkin Pie
Edna Tolliver Hayes Hollandsworth

1-1/2 cups pumpkin, cooked or canned
1 cup evaporated milk
1 cup sugar
¼ teaspoon salt
2 eggs, slightly beaten
1 tablespoon butter or margarine, melted
1 tablespoon pumpkin pie spice (see below)

Combine ingredients and mix thoroughly.
Pour into uncooked pastry-lined pie pan.
Bake in hot oven – 425 degrees – about 25 minutes or until jelled in center.

Pumpkin Pie Spice

½ teaspoon nutmeg
½ teaspoon ginger
¼ teaspoon cloves
1 teaspoon cinnamon

Mix thoroughly.

Equals 1 tablespoon pumpkin pie spice

Libby's Famous Pumpkin Pie
From the Libby Pure Pumpkin Label

1-1/2 cups granulated sugar
1 teaspoon salt
2 teaspoons ground cinnamon
1 teaspoon ground ginger
½ teaspoon ground cloves
4 eggs
3-1/2 cups Libby's Pure Pumpkin (29 ounces)
3 cups evaporated milk (two 12-ounce cans)
2 9-inch deep-dish pie shells (unbaked)

Combine sugar, salt, cinnamon, ginger and clove in medium bowl.

Beat eggs lightly in large bowl.
Stir in pumpkin and sugar/spice mixture.

Gradually stir in evaporated milk.
Pour into pie shells.

Bake in preheated 425-degree oven for 15 minutes.

Reduce temperature to 350 degrees and bake for 40 to 50 minutes or until knife inserted near center comes out clean.

Cool on wire rack for 2 hours.

Note from Helen: I use my mixer to mix up the pumpkin pie. Combines all the ingredients easier and better!

Crustless Pumpkin Pie

kimbensen.com

15 ounce can pumpkin
¾ cup Splenda®
¼ cup Egg Beaters®
1 cup nonfat milk
½ teaspoon salt
1 tablespoon flour
2 teaspoons pumpkin pie spice

Beat all ingredients together.

Spray pie plate with cooking spray.

Pour batter into pie plate and bake for 15 minutes at 400 degrees.

Reduce heat to 350 degrees and bake for an additional 45 minutes.

Place in microwave and cook on high for an additional 5 minutes.

Knife should come out clean when inserted into the center.

Allow it to cool completely before cutting it.

Top with dollop of fat-free whipped topping.

Shoo Fly Pie
Martha Lou Feeser Buskirk

1-1/2 cup flour
½ cup sugar
½ teaspoon nutmeg
1 teaspoon cinnamon
1/8 teaspoon salt
1/3 cup butter or margarine
¾ cup molasses
¾ cup water
½ teaspoon soda
1 9-inch unbaked pie shell

Sift together flour, sugar, nutmeg, cinnamon and salt.

Add butter and cut in with 2 knives or pastry blender to resemble coarse crumbs.

Combine molasses, water and soda.

Pour molasses mixture into unbaked pie shell

Spoon crumbs over top.

Bake at 375 degrees for approximately 35 minutes.

Snickers Bar Pie

Mary Etta Roth
Grateful Grubb Family Restaurant
412 South Madison Avenue
North Vernon, IN 47265
812-346-0004

8-ounce package cream cheese, softened
½ cup chunky peanut butter
1 cup powdered sugar
8-ounce container Cool Whip
13 fun-sized Snickers bars, chopped
1/3 cup milk chocolate chips
Graham cracker crust

Beat cream cheese, peanut butter and powdered sugar together with mixer until smooth and creamy.

Add Cool Whip and fold in the chopped Snickers bars and milk chocolate chips.

Spread in graham cracker crust.

Chill at least 3 hours.

Strawberry Pie
Edna Tolliver Hayes Hollandsworth

Fresh strawberries
2 tablespoons cornstarch
¾ cup sugar
¼ teaspoon salt
1 cup water
Red food coloring
Baked pie shell

Combine cornstarch, sugar, salt, water and red food coloring and cook till mixture is clear and thick.

Place as many fresh berries as you desire in baked pie shell.

Pour mixture over berries covering all of the berries.

Serve with whipped topping.

Fresh Strawberry Pie
Phyllis Lauderback

1 package strawberry Jell-O
1 cup sugar
2 tablespoons cornstarch
2 cups water
1 baked pie shell

Mix all ingredients in saucepan.

Cook until clear and beginning to thicken.

Cool until thickened.

Pour over whole or halved strawberries in a baked pie crust.

Served with whipped cream or Cool Whip topping.

Sugar Cream Pie - #1
From an Old Mennonite Cookbook

1 cup white sugar
2/3 cup brown sugar
½ cup flour
1 cup boiling water
½ pint whipping cream
1 teaspoon vanilla

Mix sugars and flour.

Mix with boiling water.

Beat well.

Add whipping cream and vanilla.

Pour into 9-inch unbaked pie shell.

Bake at 450 degrees for 10 minutes.

Reduce oven temperature to 350 degrees and bake for 30 minutes.

Sugar Cream Pie - #2
From an Old Mennonite Cookbook

½ cup flour
½ cup brown sugar
½ cup white sugar
Pinch of salt
1 cup whipping cream
1 cup milk
1 teaspoon vanilla
1 9-inch unbaked pie shell

Mix ingredients in order given.

Add the liquid slowly using a wire whisk.

Pour into unbaked 9-inch pastry shell.

Bake at 425 for 15 minutes.

Reduce temperature to 350 degrees and continue baking for 45 minutes, or until done.

Notes:

PUDDINGS

Apple Harvest Bread Pudding

Greg & Kim Evans
Crossroads Family Restaurant & Gift Shop
615 West Highway 50
Versailles, IN   47042

2 lbs. day old sour dough bread
1 quart heavy cream
1 cup whole milk
2 cups sugar
6 eggs, lightly beaten
2 tablespoons pumpkin pie spice
2 teaspoons cinnamon
1 cup pecans
2 small cans of pie apples

Slice day old bread into ¼ slices and put in large mixing bowl.
In separate bowl, combine heavy cream and milk.
Add sugar and eggs.
Add pumpkin pie spice and cinnamon.

Whisk together well until incorporated.
Add pecans and apples.
Mix together.

Pour mixture over bread and mix well until all bread is wet.

Place in 9x13 buttered pan.

Bake for 1-1/2 hours at 300 degrees.

Serve with ice cream and a warm caramel sauce.

Custard Bread Pudding
Zell Tolliver Owens Ennis

2 cups stale bread
4 cups milk, scalded
¾ cup sugar
1 tablespoon butter
¼ teaspoon salt
4 eggs, slightly beaten
1 teaspoon vanilla

Soak bread in milk for 5 minutes.
Add sugar, butter and salt.
Pour over eggs, add vanilla.
Mix well.

Pour into greased 1-1/2 quart baking dish.
Set in a pan of water and bake at 350 degrees until firm.

Vanilla Sauce

¼ cup butter
1 tablespoon cornstarch
2 tablespoons sugar
1 cup water
½ teaspoon vanilla

Mix sugar and corn starch.
Add water and bring to a boil.

If not thick enough, add more corn starch.

Add butter and vanilla when thick enough.

Pour over Bread Pudding.

Custard Bread Pudding (cont'd)

Author's Note: Although this was one of the few treats, they had, Daughter Norma remembers the Bread Pudding being the very best special treat. She has yet to taste bread pudding, biscuits or flaky, tender pies that could measure up to her Mom's. Norma also remembers a treat when Aunt Zell would open a can of blue plums, put one or two of them in individual dishes and pour the plum juice over them. However, when she makes the Bread Pudding following her Mom's recipe or even opens a can of plums and pours the juice over each serving, they simply do not taste the same as when her Mom served them.

Ruby's Bread Pudding
Ruby Tolliver Brewster

½ loaf of white bread
4 cups milk
4 or 5 eggs, beaten
1 tablespoon vanilla
1-1/2 cups sugar
1 teaspoon cinnamon

Crumble bread into a 9x13 baking dish.
Combine milk, eggs, vanilla, sugar and cinnamon.
Pour over crumbled bread.

Bake at 350-400 degrees for 30 minutes or until knife comes out clean.

Remove from oven.

Topping:

2 cups milk
1 teaspoon vanilla
1 tablespoon butter
1 cup sugar
2 tablespoons cornstarch

Combine all ingredients and cook until it thickens.
It will be less thick than pie filling

Pour over pudding.

Sprinkle with nutmeg and ENJOY!

Mother's Swedish Chocolate Pudding
Hans Johansen, Jr.

2/3 cup sugar
¼ cup cocoa
1 egg, beaten
1 cup milk
1 tablespoon or 1 envelope plain gelatin
1/4 cup water
1 cup whipping cream
1 teaspoon vanilla

Combine sugar and cocoa.
Combine beaten egg and milk and add to sugar mixture.

Cook in a heavy saucepan until mixture begins to thicken like custard.
Remove from heat before it curdles.

Dissolve gelatin in water.
Add gelatin and vanilla to cooked mixture.
Cool.

Whip the cream and fold into the cooked mixture.

Spoon into stemmed goblets or dessert dishes.

Chill.

Cinnamon Pudding
From an Old Mennonite Cookbook

1 cup sugar
2 tablespoons butter
2 teaspoons baking powder
2 cups flour
1 teaspoon cinnamon
1 cup milk

Mix above ingredients and put in bottom of a 9" x13" baking dish.

1-1/2 cups brown sugar
1-1/2 cups water
2 tablespoons butter

Boil these ingredients and pour slowly over batter in baking dish.

If desired, ½ cup raisins and ½ cup chopped nuts may be sprinkled on top.

Bake 20 to 30 minutes at 375 to 400 degrees till done.

Dirt Dessert
Helen Salyer Perkins Johansen

1/2 cup butter or margarine (room temperature)
1 package cream cheese (8 ounces)
1 large package instant vanilla pudding mix
1 large container Cool Whip
1 large package Oreo cookies (do not use Double Stuff Oreos)

Mix butter or margarine and cream cheese with a mixer.
In another bowl, prepare instant pudding as instructed on box.
Allow pudding to thicken.
Combine thickened pudding with Cool Whip.
Combine pudding mixture with butter/cream cheese mixture.

Crush Oreo cookies in food processer.
Texture should feel like potting soil.

Line a large flower pot with foil.
Fill flower pot with alternating layers of pudding and crushed cookies, finishing with a cookie layer.
Insert an artificial flower in top of pot.
Place gummy worm candy around the flower as if they were crawling out of the dirt1

Refrigerate.

Finish off the "Flower Pot" with a pretty ribbon.

Float Dessert
Willa Tolliver Salyer Lyons

2 cups milk
½ cup sugar
3 eggs (separate yolks from whites)
3 tablespoons flour
¼ teaspoon vanilla
Vanilla wafers

In a saucepan, combine sugar and flour.
Add milk, egg yolks and vanilla.
Cook over low heat until mixture thickens.
Remove from heat.
Beat egg whites until stiff.
Fold egg whites gently into cooked pudding.

Cover bottom of clear serving dish or sherbet dishes with vanilla wafers.
Pour half of the float onto the vanilla wafers.
Stand vanilla wafers around side of dish.
Pour remaining float into dish.
Roll several vanilla wafers with rolling pin.
Top float with the crushed wafers.

Chill and serve.

If float is going to be served right away, sliced bananas can be added in the bottom with the vanilla wafers and also on the top of the float. However, bananas do turn brown if not eaten pretty soon. Another idea is to add the sliced bananas to the top when you are ready to serve the float. Slices can be inserted on top of each serving.

Peanut Butter Pudding
Mona Eble Plumer

1/3 cup sugar
4-1/2 teaspoons cornstarch
½ teaspoon salt
1-1/2 cups milk
½ cup half & half cream
½ cup creamy peanut butter
1 teaspoon vanilla extract

In a saucepan, combine sugar, cornstarch and salt.

Gradually stir in milk and cream.

Bring to a boil over medium heat.

Cook and stir for 2 minutes.

Remove from heat.

Stir in peanut butter and vanilla until smooth.

Pour into small serving bowls and refrigerate.

Garnish with whipped cream, if desired.

Yield: 4 servings

Creamy Vanilla Pudding
Hans Johansen, Jr.

¼ cup corn starch
1/3 cup sugar
2 cups milk
2 eggs, slightly beaten
2 tablespoons butter or margarine
1 teaspoon vanilla

In a medium-sized glass bowl, combine cream corn starch and sugar.
With a whisk, gradually stir milk into the cream corn starch mixture.

Cook in microwave on High for 5-7 minutes or until thickened and bubbling, stirring after each 2-minute interval.

Beat half of the hot mixture into the eggs.
Blend this egg mixture into the remaining hot mixture.

Microwave on High for 1-1/2 to 2-1/2 minutes, or until thickened and heated through, stirring after each 45 seconds of cooking.

With whisk, stir in butter and vanilla.

Pour into dessert dishes.

Cover and refrigerate until chilled.

Servings: 4

Homemade Vanilla Float
Versa Tolliver Smith

6 cups milk
5 tablespoons flour, heaping
1 teaspoon salt
1-1/2 cups sugar
3 eggs
2 teaspoons vanilla
Yellow food coloring

Separate egg yolks from egg whites.
Mix dry ingredients together.
Add egg yolks.
Mix well.
Add milk and blend well.

Put on stove on low heat and stir until thick.

Pour into casserole dish.

Beat egg whites and spread over mixture.

Refrigerate or eat warm over biscuits.

Great treat for the family.

If you prefer chocolate, add 5 tablespoons Hershey's Cocoa and omit yellow food coloring.

SALADS

Alice's Deviled Eggs
Alice Ogez Litzy Perkins

6 eggs boiled hard
3 heaping teaspoons Miracle Whip
¼ teaspoon yellow mustard
2 pinches sugar
Paprika

Boil eggs 20-25 minutes once water starts to boil.
Peel eggs, cut in half length ways and place on a plate.

Put yolks in a separate bowl.
Mash yolks with fork until broken up fine.
Add 3 heaping teaspoons (use a kitchen spoon) of Miracle Whip.
Add more if needed to achieve a stiff but creamy consistency.
Add mustard. Taste and adjust mustard as needed. You just want a hint of mustard taste.
Add sugar and adjust for taste. Do not want too much sourness.

Once filling is to taste, fill egg halves with mixture.

Just before serving, sprinkle with Paprika.

Broccoli-Cauliflower Salad
Martha Lou Feeser Buskirk

5 cups broccoli florets
5 cups cauliflower pieces
2 cups shredded cheddar cheese
2/3 cup onion, chopped
½ cup raisins
1 cup mayonnaise
½ cup sugar
2 tablespoons cider or red wine vinegar
6 strips bacon, cooked and crumbled
¼ cup sunflower seeds

In a large bowl, toss broccoli, cauliflower, cheese, onion and raisins.

In a small bowl, combine mayonnaise, sugar and vinegar.

Pour over salad and toss to coat.

Cover and refrigerate for 1 hour.

Sprinkle with bacon crumbles and sunflower seeds.

Yield: 12-16 servings

Rockin' Broccoli Salad
Helen Salyer Perkins Johansen

½ cup light mayonnaise
2 packets Stevia
2 teaspoons white vinegar
1/3 cup diced red onions
2 tablespoons Real Bacon Bits

6 cups broccoli florets, uncooked
¼ cup chopped walnuts

Combine first five ingredients.

Add broccoli and mix to coat.

Top with walnuts.

Refrigerate 1 hour.

Memphis Mustard Cole Slaw
Group Recipes.com

1 bag cole slaw mix or 3-4 cups shredded cabbage
½ green pepper, seeded and finely chopped
2 tablespoons celery seed
Hot sauce

Toss together all salad ingredients.

Dressing:

¼ cup prepared yellow mustard
¼ cup apple cider vinegar
½ cup freshly squeezed lemon juice
1-1/2 cups sugar
Salt and pepper

Whisk together mustard, vinegar, lemon juice and sugar until the sugar has dissolved.

Season with salt and pepper.

Add dressing to taste and gently toss until well combined.

Season with hot sauce to taste.

Super Cole Slaw
Joan Neuenschwander Schug

¼ teaspoon pepper
½ teaspoon dry mustard
1 teaspoon celery seed
2 tablespoons sugar
¼ cup chopped green pepper
1 teaspoon salt
1 tablespoon chopped red pepper
½ teaspoon grated onion
3 tablespoons oil
1/3 cup vinegar
3 cups chopped cabbage

Place ingredients in a large bowl in the order they are listed above.

Mix well.

Cover and chill for several hours.

Last Minute Cranberry Relish
Joan Neuenschwander Schug

1 can whole cranberry sauce (16 ounces)
1 can crushed pineapple, drained (8-1/4 ounces)
¼ cup chopped pecans
¼ teaspoon apple pie spice
Pinch of ground cloves

Pour cranberry sauce into glass dish.

Add remaining ingredient and stir well to mix.

Serve at once or refrigerate until ready to serve.

Cranberry Salad
Priscilla Pyles Huff

1 package cranberries, finely chopped
10-1/2 ounce bag miniature marshmallows (white)
1-1/2 cups sugar
½ - 1 cup pecans, chopped
1 can crushed pineapple, drained
1 8-ounce container of Cool Whip

Mix cranberries, pecans, sugar and pineapple.

Refrigerate overnight.

Add marshmallows and Cool Whip at least 1 hour before serving.

Also, can freeze, but we have never had enough left to freeze so cannot report on this! Ha!

Note: This is a very old recipe that was served in the lunchroom at Cross Plains, Indiana, school. This recipe was reported by one of the cooks – my Step-Grandmother, Sylvia Mathews. She was a cook there before 1960, but I'm not sure what years. I have made this recipe every year at Thanksgiving and Christmas since 1970. My children and grandchildren insist on it. They call it Pink Stuff!

Thanksgiving Cranberry Mold
Dorcas Neidig

¾ cup boiling water
1 3-ounce package cherry Jell-O
½ cup pecans, chopped
1/3 cup celery, chopped
1 16-ounce can whole cranberry sauce
1 8-1/2 ounce can crushed pineapple, undrained

Mix water with Jell-O until dissolved.

Stir in remaining ingredients and pour into mold.

Refrigerate until firm.

Double recipe for a 9x13 cake pan.

Crisp Cucumbers
Dorcas Neidig

1-1/2 cups cold water
1-1/2 cups white vinegar
1-1/2 cups sugar
1-1/2 tablespoons onion flakes
¾ teaspoon salt
½ teaspoon garlic salt
½ teaspoon onion salt
½ teaspoon celery salt
4 medium cucumbers, sliced

Place everything in a jar except cucumbers.

Cover and shake until sugar dissolves.

Add cucumbers, cover and refrigerate.

Dee Dee's Wedding Salad
Mary Keller Kost and Bob Keller

8 ounces Cool Whip
16 ounces sour cream, softened
3-ounce package orange gelatin
Half of a 10.5-ounce package miniature marshmallows
15-ounce can crushed pineapple, well drained
11-ounce can of mandarin oranges, drained well (save juice)
6-ounce can frozen orange juice concentrate, thawed

Combine Cool Whip and sour cream until smooth.
Stir in gelatin until well mixed.
Blend in marshmallows.
Add pineapple and mandarin oranges.
Stir gently until well combined.
Add frozen juice concentrate.

Refrigerate a few hours or overnight.

Test consistency.
If too thick, add some of the mandarin orange juice.

Serves 12

Five Cup Salad
Joan Neuenschwander Schug

1 cup mandarin oranges, drained
1 cup pineapple tidbits, drained
1 cup seedless grapes
1 cup miniature marshmallows
1 cup sour cream
Shredded coconut, if desired

Thoroughly mix together all ingredients.

Cover and chill overnight or for several hours.

Frozen Fruit Salad
Geraldine Green Miracle

1 cup sour cream
½ of a 4-1/2 ounce carton whipped dessert topping (Cool Whip)
½ cup sugar
2 tablespoons lemon juice
1 teaspoon vanilla
1 can (13-ounce) crushed pineapple, drained
2 medium bananas, sliced
½ cup red candied cherries, sliced (can use the candied mixed fruit)
½ cup walnuts, chopped

In mixing bowl, blend together sour cream, dessert topping, sugar and vanilla.

Pour lemon juice over bananas and toss.

Fold in fruit and nuts.

Turn into a 4-1/2 cup ring mold.

Freeze several hours or overnight.

Unmold on lettuce-lined plate.

Garnish with additional red candied cherries, if desired.

Let stand 10 minutes before serving. Makes 8 servings.

Note: If using a Tupperware mold, make 1-1/2 times the recipe. Double the recipe for a Bundt pan.

Green Whipped Salad
kimbensen.com

1 package fat-free, sugar-free instant pistachio pudding mix
16-ounce can crushed pineapple, drained
8-ounce container fat-free whipped topping
8-ounce container fat-free cottage cheese

Mix all ingredients together.

Refrigerate for 2-3 hours.

This salad can also double as a dessert.

So yummy!!!

Jell-O Salad
Burline Meddock (Mrs. Steve) Tolliver

1 large box lime Jell-O
2 cups hot water
1 small box lemon Jell-O
1 cup hot water
½ lb. miniature marshmallows
3 small packages cream cheese, softened
1 cup pineapple juice
½ cup Miracle Whip
1 cup crushed pineapple, drained
½ pint Cool Whip
1 large box cherry Jell-O

Layer One:
Mix lime Jell-O with 2 cups hot water in a 9x13 casserole.
Allow to mold in refrigerator.

Layer Two:
Mix balance of ingredients except the Cool Whip and cherry Jell-O
Fold in Cool Whip.
Pour over molded lime Jell-O.
Let it set in refrigerator until molded.

Layer Three:
When above mixture is set, mix 1 large box cherry Jell-O with 2 cups hot water.
Let cool completely and pour over already molded mixture.

Let set in refrigerator until molded.

Ralph's Wilted Lettuce
Ralph Perkins

1 head of lettuce
6 - 8 slices of bacon
Salt and pepper

Fry bacon in large skillet until bacon is crisp.

Wash lettuce and cut up into rough pieces.
Place lettuce in large mixing bowl.

Remove bacon slices from skillet and crumble.
Pour bacon grease over lettuce.
Stir grease and lettuce together vigorously.

Add salt and pepper to taste.

Add crumbled bacon back to top of mixture.

Serve as a quick side dish.

Louisiana Carrot Salad
From an Old Mennonite Cookbook

1 cup shredded carrots
½ cup raisins
½ cup peanuts
1 tablespoon mayonnaise, or more
1 tablespoon peanut butter, or more

Simmer raisins in water to cover 5 minutes.

Use water from drained raisins to thin mayonnaise and peanut butter.

Mix ingredients and dressing just before serving.

Grandma Phyllis' Macaroni Salad
Jessica Green Ward

16-ounce box elbow macaroni
1 cup Miracle Whip
¼ cup sugar
½ small jar sweet relish
5 hardboiled eggs
1 medium onion, chopped
Small amount of milk

Boil elbow macaroni until tender, drain and cool.

Mix Miracle Whip, sugar, sweet relish, onion and enough milk to make mixture creamy.

Add elbow macaroni and eggs.

Note: My Grandma made this macaroni salad for everything, and I could never really understand why until I became an adult. Our family has always been massive and to feed us all is a challenge. So, with this recipe you can feed multitudes of people with little effort. Only difficult thing about all her recipes is there was nothing ever written down to follow. It was simply by taste!

Sweet Amish Macaroni Salad
Susan Matthews Wisecup

1 lb. macaroni
4 hard-boiled eggs, chopped
1 small onion, finely diced
3 celery ribs, diced small
1 small sweet pepper, seeded and diced small (red or orange)

Dressing:

2 cups light mayonnaise (do not use Miracle Whip)
½ cup sugar
1/8 cup yellow mustard
2 tablespoons dill pickle relish
1 tablespoon white or apple cider vinegar
3/4 teaspoon celery seed
¼ teaspoon salt
Paprika (to garnish)

Cook the macaroni according to directions and drain well.
While macaroni is cooking, mix up all the dressing ingredients until well blended and set aside.
Chop up all the veggies.

When the macaroni has cooled and drained well, mix in the dressing.

Note: Add all of the dressing if you like a very creamy salad. If you don't like a lot of dressing, leave out about ½ cup of the dressing. Remember, that as it sets, it will soak up some of the dressing.

Refrigerate for at least one hour. The longer you let it set, the better the flavor! Overnight is not too long.

Note: Recipe taken from Food.com

Pasta Salad
Mary Keller Kost

1 lb. angel hair pasta
2 tablespoons seasoned salt
1-1/2 tablespoons Accent seasoning
2/3 cup lemon juice
2/3 cup oil
¾ cup onion, finely chopped
1-1/2 cups celery, finely chopped
1 small can black olives, chopped
1 cup mayonnaise
¾ cup green peppers, optional

Cook pasta and drain.

Mix pasta, seasoned salt, Accent, lemon juice and oil together.

Let marinate 1-2 days.

Mix onions, celery, olives and mayonnaise together.

Add to pasta marinate.

Pasta Salad is ready to eat!

Overnight Salad
Joan Neuenschwander Schug

1 head lettuce, cut up (dried well)
1 large Bermuda onion, thinly sliced
1 lb. bacon, fried and broken into pieces
1 head cauliflower, cut into small pieces
¼ cup sugar
2 cups mayonnaise
1/3 cup grated Parmesan cheese
Salt and pepper to taste

Prepare the night before.

In large salad bowl, put all lettuce in first.

Add onion in next layer.

Bacon in next layer.

Cauliflower in last layer.

Sprinkle rest of ingredients, except mayonnaise, on top.

Put mayonnaise on in spoonfuls.

Cover bowl tightly and refrigerate.

Stir before serving.

Pea Salad
Bertha Tolliver Snyder

1 cup green onions, chopped
1 cup celery, chopped
1 small green pepper, chopped
1 small can Leseur peas, drained
1 small can shoepeg corn, drained
1 small jar pimentos, drained
1 small can French cut green beans, drained
1 tablespoon water
¾ cup vinegar
½ cup salad oil
1 cup sugar
1 teaspoon salt
1 teaspoon pepper

Place water, vinegar, salad oil, sugar, salt and pepper in pan and bring to a boil.
Allow to cool.

Mix onions, celery, green pepper, peas, corn, pimentos and green beans.

Pour cooled liquid over all the vegetables and stir very well.
Chill.

Serve with a slotted spoon.

Very good for carry-in dinners.

Old Fashioned Perfection Salad
From an Old Mennonite Cookbook

2 envelopes unflavored gelatin
½ cup sugar
½ cup vinegar
1 teaspoon salt
1-1/2 cups boiling water
1-1/2 cups cold water
2 tablespoons lemon juice
2 cups shredded cabbage
1 cup chopped celery
¼ cup chopped green pepper
1/3 cup stuffed olive slices

Combine first seven ingredients and chill till partially set.

Add the rest of the ingredients and pour into an 8-1/2 x 4-1/2 x 2-1/2 inch loaf pan.

Chill until firm.

Just before serving, unmold and slice into 8 to 10 pieces.

Garnish.

Pass a bowl of mayonnaise.

This is a perfect salad with most meats because of its tangy and crunchy taste and texture.

Pretzel Salad
Darla Huff Groves

1 cup crushed pretzels
1/3 cup sugar
1 stick butter
8-ounce cream cheese
½ cup sugar
20-ounce crushed pineapple, drained
8-ounce Cool Whip

Mix first three ingredients.

Bake at 400-degrees on cookie sheet for 7 minutes.

Stir and set aside to cool.

Mix balance of ingredients in large bowl.

Add cooled pretzel mix.

Chill at least one hour, preferably overnight, and serve.

Hot Spinach Salad
Hans Johansen, Jr.

3 tablespoons Wesson oil
2 tablespoons vinegar
2 teaspoons sugar
1 teaspoon lemon juice
¼ teaspoon garlic juice
1 dash Worcestershire sauce
4 strips bacon
Spinach leaves

Heat all ingredients except bacon in a fry pan until boiling.

Cook bacon crisp and break into bits.

Pour dressing over spinach leaves.

Add crumbled bacon.

Toss and serve while warm.

Servings: 2

Thousand Island Dressing
Helen Salyer Perkins Johansen

½ cup mayonnaise
2 tablespoons ketchup
1 tablespoon vinegar
2 teaspoons sugar
2 teaspoons sweet relish
1 teaspoon onion, minced
1/8 teaspoon salt
Dash of pepper

Combine all ingredients and refrigerate.

Three Layer Jell-O Salad
Bertha Tolliver Snyder

1st Layer:

Dissolve a 3-ounce package lime Jell-O in 1-1/4 cups boiling water.
Stir until thoroughly dissolved.
Add 1 cup crushed pineapple with the juice.
Let set in refrigerator until firm.

2nd Layer:

Dissolve a 3-ounce package lemon Jell-O in 1-1/4 cups boiling water.
Stir, then add a 3-ounce package of Philadelphia Cream Cheese, softened, and 1 envelope of Dream Whip made by directions on the package.
Mix together and pour over the first layer.
Let set.

3rd Layer:

Dissolve a 3-ounce package orange Jell-O in 1-1/4 cups boiling water.
Cool.
Add 1 can Mandarin oranges with the juice.
Pour over the second layer.
Chill until firmly set.

Serve on lettuce. Top with mayonnaise if desired.

Serves 12 to 15 people.

Notes:

SANDWICHES

Grilled Peanut Butter
Angela Huff Spurgeon

2 slices of bread
Peanut butter, creamy or crunchy
Butter or cooking spray
Chocolate chips, mini marshmallows, raisins – optional

Spread peanut butter on bread to make a peanut butter sandwich as normal.

Sprinkle with optional ingredients if desired.

Melt butter in skillet or spray with cooking spray.

Add sandwich to skillet and toast both sides like a grilled cheese sandwich.

Note: This recipe was created when my kids were little and had friends over and I needed to fix a quick lunch. I ran out of cheese for grilled cheese sandwiches and wondered if I could possibly grill a peanut butter sandwich. Peanut butter on toast is a favorite of mine so I gave it a try. It was a huge hit with my son's friend and he went home raving to his mom about the fantastic lunch that I had fixed for them. Necessity really is the mother of invention!

SNACKS

Cheese Straws – Puff Pastry Strips
Mom's Old Green Recipe Book

2 cups sifted flour
2 teaspoons baking powder
1 teaspoon salt
½ cup butter
¼ teaspoon paprika or red pepper
1 egg
½ cup milk
¾ cup grated cheese

Mix flour, salt, baking powder and paprika or red pepper.

Sift these ingredients three times.

Put in mixing bowl, chop in butter and drop in unbeaten egg.

Add cheese and milk and mix together.

Turn out on wooden board or counter.

Roll out 1/8-inch thick.

Cut into 4-inch long and ¼-inch wide sticks.

Bake in moderate (350) oven until light brown.

Fried Cheerios
Derek Holliday

2-3 cups Cheerios
1 tablespoon butter or margarine

Melt butter or margarine in iron skillet.

Add Cheerios and heat.

Makes a wonderful snack!

Steven's Haystacks
Alice Ogez Litzy Perkins

1 bag of Chow Mein noodles
1 large bag of white chocolate chips
2 large mixing bowls
Aluminum foil or wax paper.

Place noodles in one bowl.
Place white chocolate chips in another bowl.
Spread aluminum foil or wax paper over a large area on counter.
Place white chocolate chips in microwave.
Heat chocolate in 15-second intervals in microwave. Stop and stir at intervals.
Continue cooking until chocolate is creamy.
Pour melted chocolate over chow mein noodles and mix quickly.
Easiest to do with gloved hands.

Grab pinches out of mixture and loosely make haystacks on aluminum foil.

Allow to cool before serving.

My son, Steven, loved these and asked for them long before Thanksgiving. He expected us to have them all through the holidays!

Hidden Valley Ranch Oyster Crackers
Joan Neuenschwander Schug

¾ cup salad oil
1 envelope Hidden Valley Original Ranch Salad Dressing Mix
½ teaspoon dill weed
¼ teaspoon lemon pepper
¼ teaspoon garlic powder
12 16-ounce packages plain oyster crackers

Whisk together first five ingredients.

Pour over crackers, stirring to coat.

Place on baking sheet(s) and bake at 275 degrees for 15-20 minutes.

Popcorn Balls
Ruby Brady (Mrs. Leck) Tolliver

5 quarts popped corn
2 cups sugar
1-1/2 cups water
½ cup white corn syrup
¼ teaspoon salt
1 teaspoon vanilla
1 teaspoon vinegar

Combine sugar, water, syrup, salt, vanilla and vinegar.

Stir only until sugar dissolves.

Cook in saucepan to hard ball setting on candy thermometer (270 degrees).

Add popcorn and QUICKLY form into balls.

Note: It is good to have a pan of cold water to keep rinsing hands as this mixture is very hot!

Makes 40-50 balls the size of tennis balls.

Praline Pecan Crunch
Helen Salyer Perkins Johansen

1 16-ounce package Quaker® Oat Squares cereal (8 cups)
2 cups pecan pieces
½ cup light corn syrup
½ cup firmly packed brown sugar
¼ cup margarine (1/2 stick)
1 teaspoon vanilla
½ teaspoon baking soda

Heat oven to 250 degrees.
Combine cereal and pecans in a 9x13 pan; set aside.

Combine corn syrup, brown sugar and margarine in a 2-cup microwaveable bowl.

Microwave on High 1-1/2 minutes; stir.

Microwave on High ½ to 1-1/2 minutes more or until boiling.

Stir in vanilla and baking soda and pour over cereal mixture. Stir to coat evenly.

Bake 1 hour, stirring every 20 minutes.

Spread on baking sheet to cool.

Break into pieces.

Makes 10 cups.

Puppy Chow
Dorcas Neidig

1 stick margarine
1 cup peanut butter
1 cup chocolate chips
9 cups Crispix cereal
2 cups powdered sugar

Melt margarine, peanut butter and chocolate chips.

Pour over the cereal.

Put powdered sugar in a large closed container.

Add cereal mixture and shake until the cereal is coated with powdered sugar.

Southwestern Black Bean Salsa
Geraldine Green Miracle

1 can (15 ounce) black beans, rinsed and drained
1 can white shoepeg corn
1 medium tomato, chopped
   (may substitute canned tomatoes, drained and chopped)
½ cup red onion, chopped
½ cup green pepper, chopped
½ teaspoon garlic powder

Dressing:

½ cup fat free Italian salad dressing
2 teaspoons fresh cilantro, chopped
   (may substitute dried cilantro, but it takes more than fresh)
3/4 teaspoon hot pepper sauce (Tabasco)
½ teaspoon chili powder

Mix dressing and pour over vegetables.

Cover and refrigerate for at least two (2) hours before serving.

This is great served with Baked Tostitos chips!

Spiced Pecans

Lori Means Underwood
Classic Stained Glass & Gift Gallery
250 Hoosier Street
North Vernon, IN 47265
812-346-4527

1 egg white
2 tablespoons water
1 cup sugar
1 teaspoon salt
1 teaspoon cinnamon
1 lb. pecans

Beat egg white with water until frothy.

Add pecans and stir until they are coated.

In separate container, mix sugar, salt and cinnamon.

Pour over pecans and stir until well coated again.

Pour pecans onto greased cookie sheet and bake at 350 degrees for 30-40 minutes.

Stir every 10-15 minutes.

Take it out and eat it!!

Stuffed Celery
Priscilla Pyles Huff

1 8-ounce cream cheese, softened
2 beef bouillon cubes
2 teaspoon hot water
1 tablespoon fresh onion, minced
1 package celery

Dissolve bouillon in water.

Add to cream cheese and mix.

Add a little milk if mixture is too thick.

Stuff celery and cut in serving size.

Trail Mix
Connor Ambrose Perkins, age 4

In mixing bowl, combine equal part of dried fruit (apples, raisins and cherries) and lightly salted peanuts.

For variety, add an equal part of Cheerios.

Mix well.

Put into Ziploc bags.

Pack into backpack.

Great with "hiker water" – water in a sports bottle!

SOUPS

Cauliflower Soup
Elaine Basham

1 medium onion
2 stalks celery
4 mushrooms
2 tablespoons oil
1 can chicken broth
1 package frozen cauliflower
1 package California mixed vegetables
Salt to taste
3 tablespoons butter
1 can cream of chicken soup
Mrs. Dash original seasoning, to taste
1 can evaporated milk
4 tablespoons flour
½ cup water
Pepper to taste

Sauté onion, celery and mushrooms in oil.
Add broth, cauliflower, mixed vegetables and salt.
Cook until desired tenderness.
Reduce heat to simmer.
Add butter, cream of chicken soup, Mrs. Dash seasoning and milk.
Mix flour and water.
Add to soup.
Add pepper to taste.

For creamier chowder consistency, add ½ cup instant potatoes.

Chester Soup
Mary Reed Pochiba

½ cup green pepper, chopped
1 cup celery, chopped
1 large can tomato juice
1 large onion, chopped
1 can diced tomatoes
1 can green beans
¼ teaspoon garlic powder
1 tablespoon parsley flakes
1 beef bouillon cube
2 teaspoons chili powder
2 teaspoons cumin

Combine all ingredients and simmer for 1 hour.

Note: I sometimes add a can of carrots or corn to make it have more veggies in it!

Alice's Chili
Alice Ogez Perkins

2 pounds of ground beef (Fattier beef will produce better finished flavor)
1 whole medium sweet onion (always look for Vidalia onions, they are the best by far)
1 large can of Red Gold tomato juice.
2 small cans (15oz.) Brooks Chili Beans, hot or mild depending on your taste
2 heaping tablespoons chili powder or more to your taste.
3-4 dried chili peppers, optional - we add them if we have them
Salt
Black pepper
Cooked macaroni or angel hair pasta, if desired

Brown ground beef. Fattier beef will produce better finished flavor.
Add salt and pepper to taste.
Dice and add onion. Always look for Vidalia onions; they are the best by far!
Cook until onions are translucent.
Add remain ingredients.
We use about half of one of the tall bottles of Mexene chili powder in each batch. Sounds like a lot but we don't use any other real spices. You can add the half bottle. It is probably more accurate measure, but it has to be a full bottle to do that.

Cook over low heat, tasting often. Flavor will change as it warms and cooks.

Serve over macaroni or angel hair pasta, if desired.

Chili
Melvin Ward (Brother-in-Law of Jessica Green Ward)

3 lbs. lean ground beef
3 15-ounce cans petite diced tomatoes
3 15-ounce cans tomato sauce
1 can light red kidney beans
1 can dark red kidney beans
1 can white kidney Bush beans
1 can black kidney beans
1 can chili beans
3 medium onions, chopped
1 green bell pepper, chopped
1 red bell pepper, chopped
1 yellow bell pepper, chopped
3 tablespoons chili powder
3 teaspoons salt
6 cups water

Brown ground beef, drain and set aside.

Brown the chopped onion and peppers.

Combine all ingredients except beans, in a large pot.

Bring to a boil, then lower the temperature and simmer for one hour.

Add kidney beans and simmer for an hour.

Serve hot with shredded cheese.

Chili Con Carne
Priscilla Pyles Huff

1 lb. ground beef
1 onion, chopped
½ green pepper, chopped
1 can mushrooms, drained saving liquid
1 clove garlic, minced
¾ cup mushroom liquid (add enough water to the mushroom liquid to make ¾ cup)
1 teaspoon powdered beef bouillon
1 can red beans, undrained
3 teaspoons chili powder

In a skillet, sauté beef, onion, green pepper, mushrooms and garlic until beef is done.

Drain and add balance of ingredients.

Simmer 20 minutes.

Monk's Chili
From an Old Mennonite Cookbook

1 lb. hamburger
1 small onion, minced
1 large can Brooks chili beans with gravy
1 large can whole tomatoes
1 can tomato soup
Sugar, to taste
Chili powder, to taste

Brown minced onion in butter.

Add hamburger with onion and brown.

Add rest of ingredients.

If chili is too thick, add tomato juice or water.

The longer it cooks, the better it is.

Serves 6

Mushroom Salsa Chili
Lori Tolliver Holberg

1 lb. ground beef
1 lb. spicy sausage
2 16-ounce cans kidney beans, rinsed and drained
1 24-ounce jar chunky salsa
1 14.5-ounce can diced tomatoes, undrained
1 large onion, chopped
1 8-ounce can tomato sauce
1 4-ounce can mushroom stems and pieces, drained (optional)
½ cup sweet red peppers, chopped
½ cup sweet yellow peppers, chopped
½ cup sweet green peppers, chopped
½ teaspoon dried oregano
½ teaspoon garlic powder
1/8 teaspoon dried thyme
1/8 teaspoon dried marjoram

In a large skillet, brown meats over medium heat and drain.

Transfer meat to a 5-quart slow cooker.

Stir in remaining ingredients.

Cover and cook on low for 8-9 hours or until vegetables are tender.

Yield: 8 servings

Note: Lori uses alpaca meat. Venison, turkey or any other group meat could be substituted for the ground beef.

Prize-Winning Chili
John & Dana Perkins

2 pounds ground sirloin
1 package Chili-O seasoning
1 can tomato paste
1 can chili-ready diced tomatoes
2 cans Brooks Chili Beans; 1 hot & 1 mild
1 small onion
Salt and pepper to taste

Brown meat, salt and pepper with onions.

Brown until onions are tender.

Add Chili-O.

Fill empty Chili-O package with water and add to meat mixture.

Add tomato paste and stir well.

Add can of tomatoes.

Add beans and stir well.

Add water if too thick.

*Add extra chili peppers to taste.

Note: Add ingredients in order as listed.

Corn Chowder
Joan Neuenschwander Schug

5 slices bacon
1 medium onion, thinly sliced and separated into rings
2 medium potatoes, pared and diced (1-1/2 cups)
½ cup water
1 teaspoon salt
1 can cream-style corn (17 ounces)
2 cups milk
Dash of pepper
Butter

In large saucepan, cook bacon till crisp.

Remove bacon, crumble and set aside.

Reserve 3 tablespoons bacon drippings in saucepan; discard remainder.

Add onion slices to saucepan and cook till lightly browned.

Add diced potato, water and salt.

Cook over medium heat till potato is tender – 10 to 15 minutes.

Add corn, milk, pepper, crumbled bacon and a pat of butter.

Cook until heated through.

Fish Chowder
Evalyn Clutters (Mrs. Tom) Tolliver

2 cups fish, cut up
3 potatoes (size of tennis balls, cut in small pieces)
1 onion (same size as potatoes, diced)
2 tablespoons butter
1 small can evaporated milk
3 cups milk
Flour

Place fish, potatoes, onion and butter in large pot.

Add salt and pepper to taste.

Cover with water.

Boil until done. (When potatoes are tender, the rest will be also.)

Leave in pot and mix in evaporated milk.

Add 3 cups regular milk.

Bring back to boil and thicken slightly with flour and milk mixture.

Crockpot Cheesy Broccoli Potato Soup
Cathy Smith

2 bags frozen southern hash browns (little squared potatoes)
1 box chicken broth
1 can cream of chicken soup
2 16-ounce bags shredded sharp cheddar cheese
3 packages of Real bacon bits (I buy Kroger brand)
1 8-ounce package cream cheese, softened
Fresh broccoli tips

Put chicken broth in crockpot.

Add cream of chicken soup, two packages of bacon bits, broccoli, one bag of hash browns, cream cheese and three cups of cheddar cheese.

Cook on low for about 2 or 3 hours so the potatoes shrink down enough to add another bag of frozen potatoes.

Let it cook on low until cream cheese is completely melted and soup looks creamy.

Serve with remaining cheddar and bacon bits to sprinkle on top in your bowl.

Hamburger Soup
From an Old Mennonite Cookbook

1 lb. ground beef
5 cups water
1 16-ounce can tomatoes, cut up
1 cup chopped onions
1 cup sliced carrots
1 cup chopped celery
1/3 cup barley
¼ cup ketchup
1 tablespoon instant beef bouillon
2 teaspoons seasoned salt
1 teaspoon dried basil, crushed
1 bay leaf
Salt and pepper to taste

Brown beef and drain.

Add water and all other ingredients.

Bring to a boil.

Reduce heat and simmer, covered, for one hour.

Remove bay leaf before serving.

JUCA (Traditional Slovak Christmas Soup)
Larry Smeyak

Ahead of time, dry 3 lbs. fresh mushrooms.

On the day of making the soup, soak mushrooms in warm water 30-45 minutes. Drain and rinse thoroughly (2 or 3 times), chop.

The old folks used to string them up using a thread and needle and hang the string in a warm dry place for a month or longer.

I use pre-sliced white mushrooms and put them on a fine grate in the oven and dry them at 180 degrees for 4-5 hours. I then hang them in cheese cloth sacks in a warm place for a week or two before rehydrating and chopping them as described above.

3-4 lb. pork loin roast
8 quarts water
1 teaspoon black pepper
1-1/2 tablespoons salt

Place in large pot and bring to a boil. Simmer pork slowly for 1-1/4 hours.

Meanwhile cook 1-1/4 cups of barley for 15 minutes. Cover barley with water, boil for 15 minutes, drain and rinse.

Also, cook 2 lbs. kielbasa in water. Bring to a boil and boil 5-10 minutes and drain.

Remove 1 quart of broth from cooked pork roast and set aside to thin the soup later if it is too thick.

Add the mushrooms, barley and kielbasa to cooked pork roast in remaining broth.

Add one 32-ounce jar of sauerkraut, including the juice.

JUCA (cont'd)

Simmer for two hours. Remove pork roast if it is getting too well done. It can be sliced and served along with the soup or added to the soup just prior to serving.

Add more sauerkraut juice and salt to taste. Simmer 5 minutes longer.

You can sometimes find sauerkraut juice in an 8-ounce can. I usually just buy a second 32-ounce jar of sauerkraut and use some of the juice from it.

Note: My Grandmother immigrated from Czechoslovakia in the early 1900's with her infant daughter Ann, coming through Ellis Island. Grandfather was already in the states and waiting for her. Over the years they had five more daughters which they raised in a two-bedroom, one-acre farmhouse with no running water, no electricity and a coal stove for heat in the winter. She made this soup as part of a traditional Christmas Eve dinner. All the girls maintained the tradition over the years, and now it has been passed on to the grandchildren, many of whom still maintain the tradition, including myself.   Larry Smeyak

Author's Note: Larry and his wife, Rita, were seat mates of mine on a plane headed to Ft Myers, Florida in May of 2018. While discussing my recipe book, he told me about this recipe and was kind enough to allow me to include it herein. Thanks much, Larry!

Lemon Rice Soup
Kathy Lafakis

Ingredients:
½ chicken with skin
3 large lemons, room temperature
3 large eggs, room temperature
48 ounces chicken broth
1-½ cups converted rice
1 teaspoon black pepper
1 teaspoon salt

Directions:
Roll each lemon firmly on the counter to break up the lemon fiber providing more juice.
Combine chicken, salt, pepper and 3 quarts of water into a large pot.
Bring chicken to a boil covered, then cover partially to reduce the broth a bit.
Boil until the meat starts to fall off of the bone, approximately one hour.
Skim the froth off the boiling water and dispose.
Let the meat cool.
Skin and debone the chicken.
Pour the chicken broth into the pot with the existing broth and bring to a boil.
Add rice and boil covered for 20 minutes (longer for softer rice).
Crack the eggs into a separate bowl.
Squeeze the lemon juice from all three lemons and combine with the three whole eggs and blend. Cut up the chicken thoroughly.
While constantly stirring the eggs and lemon, add the broth slowly.
Pour the egg-lemon broth mixture back into the pot with rice and add the chicken.
Salt and pepper to taste and more lemon juice if desired.

Note: Add more rice if you desire a thicker soup.

Creamy Mushroom Soup
From an Old Mennonite Cookbook

¾ lb. mushrooms
¼ cup butter
¾ cup celery, finely chopped (optional)
3 tablespoons flour
½ teaspoon salt
3 13-3/4 ounce cans chicken broth
1 cup whipping cream

Wash mushrooms, trim off ends and chop coarsely.

Heat butter in 3-quart pan.

Sauté mushrooms and celery for about 5 minutes.

Sprinkle flour and salt over to coat.

Add chicken broth gradually, stirring constantly.

Bring to a boil.

Remove from heat and stir in cream.

Whip briefly in container or electric blender.

Reheat, but do not boil.

Oriental Soup
Joan Neuenschwander Schug

4 13-3/4 ounce cans chicken broth (total 55 ounces)
1-1/2 teaspoons chicken bouillon
1 10-ounce package frozen shrimp, thawed
1 6-ounce package frozen pea pods, thawed
1 cup sliced mushrooms
¼ cup sliced green onions
¼ cup chopped fresh parsley
¼ of a 1 lb. package angel hair pasta, uncooked and broken into thirds
1/8 teaspoon garlic powder
Cayenne pepper to taste

In Dutch oven, heat chicken broth and bouillon to boiling.

Add remaining ingredients.

Reduce heat and simmer 5 minutes.

DO NOT OVERCOOK

Potato Soup
Crystal Russell McClure

4 large potatoes, boiled
1 bag frozen broccoli, carrots and cauliflower
1 packet ranch seasoning
1 small block of cheese
Salt and pepper to taste
1-2 cups milk

Dump half of the water off from boiling the potatoes.

Peel and cube potatoes.

Add potatoes, broccoli, carrots, cauliflower, ranch seasoning, cheese, salt and pepper to the water saved from boiling the potatoes.

Add as much milk as desired to make the soup creamy.

Heat until hot but not boiling.

Add meat, if desired. I like smoked sausage.

Amazing soup!!

Potato Soup (Bloodmobile!)
From an Old Mennonite Cookbook

7 cups cubed potatoes (about 3 pounds)
3-4 stalks celery, chopped
1 small-to-medium onion, chopped
2/3 stick butter
1 can beef consommé
2 quarts milk
1 tablespoon salt
½ teaspoon pepper

Cook potatoes until just tender in small amount of water.

Sauté celery and onion in melted butter until clear. <u>Do not brown.</u>

Add celery-onion mixture to potatoes with salt, pepper and consommé.

Add milk and heat. <u>Do not boil.</u> Milk may be heated before adding.

Makes 15 1-cup servings.

Note: This soup was made to serve volunteers who helped with the Bloodmobile visits.

Sausage Chowder
Dana Graham Perkins

1 lb. smoked sausage, sliced
1 can corn, drained
1 can cream of potato soup
1 can mushrooms, drained
1 can sliced potatoes, drained
1 medium onion, chopped
2 ribs of celery, chopped
Butter
Milk
Pepper

In medium-size pot, sauté celery in butter till it starts to soften.

Add onion and continue to sauté till soft.
Add smoked sausage and cook till warmed through.
Add cream of potato soup and stir.
Add corn, mushrooms and sliced potatoes.

Stir gently as not to break up potatoes.

Cover to top of ingredients with milk.
Use more milk or less to your desired thickness of chowder.

Add more butter and pepper to taste.

Heat on medium until heated through.

Goes perfect with corn bread muffins!

Enjoy!

Italian Vegetable Soup
Linda Arganbright

1 lb. ground beef
1 cup diced onion
1 cup chopped celery
1 cup sliced carrots
2 cloves garlic, minced
1 can tomatoes (16 ounces)
1 can tomato sauce (15 ounces)
1 can kidney beans (15 ounces)
2 cups water
5 teaspoons beef bouillon granules
1 tablespoon dried parsley flakes
1 teaspoon salt
½ teaspoon oregano
¼ teaspoon pepper
2 cups shredded cabbage
1 cup frozen, fresh or canned green beans
½ cup uncooked small elbow macaroni
Parmesan cheese, optional

Brown the beef and drain.
Add beef and remaining ingredients except cabbage, green beans, macaroni and cheese in a large heavy pot.
Bring to a boil and simmer for 30 minutes.
Add cabbage, green beans and macaroni.
Bring to a boil, then simmer until vegetables are tender and macaroni is done.

Sprinkle with shredded Parmesan cheese, if desired, before serving.
Enjoy!

Option: Add beef broth or additional water for a thinner soup.

Vegetable Soup
Helen Salyer Perkins Johansen

½ lb. beef cubes
1 large onion, chopped
4 potatoes, cubed
2 carrots, chopped
½ cup green beans
½ cup lima beans
½ cup frozen peas
2 stalks celery, chopped
½ cup whole kernel corn
½ cup cabbage, chopped
1 small can whole tomatoes
2 small dried hot peppers
½ cup rice
Salt and pepper to taste

Place beef cubes and onion in medium sized pot with 4 cups of water.
Cook until beef can be broken apart with a fork.
Beef can be cooked under steam in pressure cooker for about 30 minutes.

Add carrots, beans, celery, corn, cabbage, tomatoes, hot peppers, salt and pepper.
Bring to a boil, cover and simmer for approximately 1 hour.

Add potatoes and rice.

Bring back to a boil, cover and simmer for 30 minutes or until potatoes are done.

Remove the hot peppers before serving.

Wonderful on cold winter days!!!

Vegetable Soup (cont'd)

Note: A package of frozen mixed vegetables can be used instead of the carrots, beans, peas and corn. Any vegetable can be omitted, or any vegetable added! Type of vegetables depends on individual tastes. When you have a few leftover vegetables or meat scraps, just freeze them for use in vegetable soup later.

VEGETABLES

Old Settler's Baked Beans
Linda Carson Ross

1 lb. bacon, cooked
2 lb. ground beef
1 medium onion
½ cup ketchup
½ cup barbecue sauce
2 tablespoons mustard
2 tablespoons molasses
1 teaspoon salt
1 16-ounce can chili beans
1 16-ounce can navy beans
1 16-ounce can butter or lima beans
2 16-ounce cans pork & beans
½ cup brown sugar

Combine all ingredients and pour into baking dish.

Bake for 1 hour at 350 degrees.

Billy's Cowboy Beans
Billy Higgs

½ lb. bacon, fried and crumbled
3 medium onions, fried in bacon grease
1 large can Bush's baked beans
1 regular can black beans, drained and washed
1 regular can northern beans, drained and washed
1 regular can navy beans, drained and washed
1 large bottle Sweet Baby Rays BBQ sauce

Combine all ingredients and simmer for at least an hour.

Beans get better every time they are reheated!!

Sweet Pickled Beets
Versa Tolliver Smith

7 cans regular sliced beets, drained
2 cups sugar
2 sticks of cinnamon
1 tablespoon whole allspice
1-1/2 teaspoons salt
3-1/2 cups vinegar
1-1/2 cups water
Boiled eggs

Combine all ingredients except beets in saucepan.

Bring to a boil, reduce heat and simmer for 5 minutes.

Throw away cinnamon sticks.

Add beets to pickle juice.

Place beets, boiled eggs and juice in jar and seal.

Let set for 2 weeks.

Microwave Corn on the Cob
Helen Salyer Perkins Johansen

4 ears fresh corn on the cob

Husk, wash and trim ears of corn.
Place cobs in a 12x7 inch glass baking dish.
Do not add any water; it's not necessary.

Cover dish of corn with plastic wrap and place in microwave.
Microwave 7 to 8 minutes on HIGH.

For 2 ears, microwave 4 to 5 minutes on HIGH.

For 6 ears, microwave 9 to 10 minutes on HIGH.

To microwave individual ears of corn, wash and wrap each ear in plastic wrap.

Microwave 3 minutes on HIGH.

Corn may seem firm when removed from oven after microwaving.

But cooking continues, so allow it to stand covered 2 to 5 minutes, depending on the number of ears being cooked.

Uncover and season as desired.

Mary's Fried Corn
Geraldine Green Miracle

6 ears fresh corn (Silver Queen works well)
½ stick butter
¾ to 1 cup water
2-3 tablespoons all-purpose flour
1-1/2 tablespoons sugar (may need a little more or less – taste)
Salt to taste (at the end of cooking)

Into a bowl, cut fresh corn off cob (barely cutting top of kernels), then with the knife scrape every bit of corn off the cob into the bowl – this is messy!

Add water and stir.

Place butter in large skillet (iron skillet if you have it; if not use a good non-stick skillet)

After butter melts, add the corn and water mixture. Let the mixture cook for 2-3 minutes.

In a separate small bowl or cup, add the flour and enough water to make a smooth paste. A wire whisk helps with this. Add just a little additional water to make the mixture so you can pour it into the corn.

Add the flour mixture to the corn/water mixture in the skillet. Stir while corn and flour mixture cook together thickening the corn.

Cook until corn is done. This only takes a few minutes.

Taste at this point and add sugar and salt to taste.

Mary's Fried Corn (cont'd)

If corn is too thick or too thin, adjust with a little more water or another small amount of flour/water paste.

Note: I watched my grandmother make this and she taught my mother to make it, then I watched her. This is the most accurate I could write the recipe from watching two great cooks make the best corn you will ever eat!

Fried Corn
Helen Salyer Perkins Johansen

6-8 ears fresh corn
2 tablespoons bacon grease or butter
1 cup water
Salt and pepper to taste

Cut corn off of cob.

It is best to make the cut about halfway into the kernels and then scrape the rest of the corn out with the side of your knife.

Add seasoning (bacon grease or butter).
Add ½ cup water, salt and pepper.

Pour into iron skillet.

Bring to a boil and cook for 5-10 minutes.

If corn is too thick, add remaining water.

Note: You can fry 2-3 slices of bacon, break it into small pieces and fry the corn in the same skillet.

Grandma Tolliver's Dill Pickles
Lou Sena Phillips Tolliver

Clean cucumbers.
Soak in cold salt water overnight.
Dry off.
Pack in jars with dill between.
Pinch of alum on top.

Combine:
Three (3) quarts water.
One (1) quart vinegar.
One (1) cup salt.

Boil.

Fill jars and seal.

Note from Grandma:

Helen, if you don't use all the mixture it will keep for another canning, or you could mix just half the recipe. It won't spoil.

Author's Note: Grandma wrote out her Dill Pickle recipe for me many years ago and it is copied herein just as she wrote it. I have framed her hand written original recipe and have it in a place of honor in my dining room. A precious treasure!

Stuffed Green Peppers
Dorcas Neidig

6 medium green peppers
½ lb. ground beef
1 small onion
1-1/2 teaspoons salt
½ teaspoon pepper
½ teaspoon garlic powder
1 cup cooked long grain rice
1 can condensed tomato soup
½ cup water
6 slices American or cheddar cheese

Cut off tops of peppers and remove seeds and membrane.

Cook ground beef with onion, salt, pepper and garlic powder.

Add cooked rice.

Fill peppers with meat mixture.
Arrange snuggly in a 3-quart casserole dish.

Mix together soup and water.
Pour over and around peppers.

Cover and microwave on high for 25 minutes.

Remove peppers and put cheese on top.

Cover and let stand for 15-20 minutes.

Pot Pie
From an Old Mennonite Cookbook

3 or 4 medium sized potatoes
2 tablespoons butter
1 teaspoon salt
1 egg
1 tablespoon water
½ cup flour
1/8 teaspoon salt

Pare potatoes; cut into ¼ inch slices.
Melt butter in a 2-quart sauce pan.
Add potatoes, 1 teaspoon salt and enough water to barely cover the potatoes.

Boil till partially done, 10 to 15 minutes.

Beat egg; add water, 1/8 teaspoon salt and flour making a dough firm enough to roll out.
Roll out on floured board or pastry cloth till it is quite thin and cut into 1-1/2 inch squares.
Drop these pieces into the saucepan with the potatoes that should be partially done now.

Continue cooking this mixture for another 10 minutes or till the dough and potatoes are done.

You may need to add some extra water when the dough is added, to finish cooking the mixture.

Variations: Beef or chicken broth may be used for the liquid.

Aunt Alice's Potatoes
Alice Neuenschwander Riegsecker
from an Old Mennonite Cookbook

2 pounds frozen hash browns
½ cup melted butter
1 teaspoon salt
1/4 teaspoon pepper
1 can cream of chicken soup, undiluted
2 cups cheddar cheese, grated
½ cup onion, chopped
2 cups sour cream
2 cups cornflakes, crushed
¼ cup melted butter

Thaw potatoes.
Combine them with the rest of the ingredients, except cornflakes and ¼ cup melted butter.

Pour potato mixture into a greased 9" x 13" dish.

Mix cornflakes and the ¼ cup melted butter and spread on top of potato mixture.

Bake at 350 degrees for 45 minutes.

You can put this into two smaller casserole dishes; bake one and freeze one.

Sloppy Fried Potatoes
Pearl Tolliver Simpson

Peel and shred as many potatoes as you need.

Brown in skillet in lard.

Add enough water to keep from sticking.

Cover and let steam until potatoes are done.

Author's Note: This recipe and her recipe for "Noodles and Tomatoes" in the Noodles/Dumplings section may seem rather plain, but during the difficult years of the Depression, Aunt Pearl made dishes such as these that did not require a lot of store-bought items yet were delicious and filling. The tomatoes and potatoes were from her garden and the eggs in the noodles were from the hen house, so all it took was her good cooking knowledge to put it all together.

Gourmet Potatoes
Hans Johansen, Jr.

6 medium potatoes, peeled and diced
2 cups shredded cheddar cheese
¼ cup butter
1-1/2 cup sour cream
1/3 cup finely chopped green onion or chives
1 teaspoon salt
¼ teaspoon pepper
2 tablespoons butter
Paprika

Cook and mash the potatoes without milk or butter.

Add cheese, butter, sour cream, onion or chives, salt and pepper.

Pour into greased 9x13 baking dish.

Dot on top with butter and sprinkle with paprika or save some of the shredded cheese and use it as the topping.

Bake uncovered at 350 degrees for 20-30 minutes.

Potato Salad
Pearl Tolliver Simpson

6 large potatoes, boiled with skins on
3 eggs, hard boiled
½ cup green onion, chopped
½ cup cucumber, chopped
¼ cup pimentos, chopped
1 teaspoon celery seed
3 tablespoons Miracle Whip salad dressing
Salt and pepper to taste

Cool and then peel the potatoes and dice in medium-sized pieces.

Peel, dice and add the hard-boiled eggs.

Add onion, cucumber, pimentos, celery seed, salt and pepper.

Combine these ingredients and stir gently with a wooden spoon.

Add Miracle Whip to the potato mixture and stir gently with a wooden spoon until well mixed.

Pour into serving bowl. Refrigerate until ready to serve.

Author's Note: Aunt Pearl always served her potato salad in a crock. For a period of time, she lived in the house at the end of the lane going up to Grandma's home. She was very particular about making fresh potato salad and didn't make it until Mother's Day morning. I can still see her hurrying into the yard with the potato salad crock in her hands, getting it to the table just moments before the Blessing was asked. Or perhaps just after. But that didn't bother anyone because the Mother's Day dinner would not be complete without Aunt Pearl's wonderful potato salad. And her beautiful sweet smile!

Potato Salad
From an Old Mennonite Cookbook

½ cup milk
1/3 cup sugar
¼ cup vinegar
1 egg
4 tablespoons butter or margarine
1 tablespoon cornstarch
¾ teaspoon salt
¾ teaspoon celery seed
¼ teaspoon dry mustard
¼ cup salad dressing
¼ cup chopped onion
6 cups cooked potatoes, peeled and diced (7 medium potatoes)
3 hard-cooked eggs, chopped

In medium sauce pan, combine milk, sugar, vinegar, egg, butter or margarine, cornstarch, salt, celery seed and dry mustard.

Cook and stir over low heat till thickened.

Remove from heat; blend in onion and salad dressing; cool.

Combine potatoes and hard-cooked eggs; carefully fold in dressing.

Chill.

Sprinkle with paprika.

Mom's Cooked Potato Salad Dressing
Hans Johansen, Jr.

1/3 cup sugar
½ teaspoon salt
¼ teaspoon dry mustard
2 tablespoons flour, rounded
1 whole egg
½ cup vinegar
½ cup water

Combine all ingredients in top of a double boiler.

Cook over low heat, stirring with a whisk until mixture begins to thicken.

Remove from heat, allow to cool.

Refrigerate until ready to use.

Potato Salad

Helen Salyer Perkins Johansen

6 boiled potatoes (cold)
3 hard-boiled eggs
¼ cup celery, finely chopped
¼ cup onion, finely chopped
1 tablespoon sweet relish
Salt and pepper to taste
3 tablespoons Miracle Whip
1 teaspoon yellow mustard
½ teaspoon sugar
1 teaspoon vinegar or dill pickle juice
1 tablespoon milk

Peel and dice the potatoes.
Dice and add two of the hard-boiled eggs.
Add relish, celery, onion, salt and pepper.
Combine ingredients gently with a wooden spoon.

In a separate bowl, combine Miracle Whip, mustard, sugar, vinegar or pickle juice and milk.
Taste.
If too sweet, add a bit more vinegar or pickle juice.
Pour dressing mixture over potato mixture and stir gently with a wooden spoon.
Pour into serving bowl and garnish with remaining boiled egg, sliced in rings.
Lightly sprinkle with paprika.
Refrigerate until ready to serve.

Did you know?? Paprika is made by grinding sweet red peppers!!

Orange Spiced Sweet Potatoes
Priscilla Pyles Huff

2 pounds sweet potatoes, peeled and sliced
½ cup dark brown sugar, packed
1 stick butter, cut in small pieces
1 teaspoon cinnamon
½ teaspoon nutmeg
½ teaspoon grated orange peel
Juice of 1 medium orange
¼ teaspoon salt
1 teaspoon vanilla
Pecans, toasted and chopped (optional)

Place all ingredients except pecans in skillet.

Cook until potatoes are tender.

Sprinkle with pecans before serving.

Candied Sweet Potatoes
Mina Elizabeth Perkins

3 lbs. sweet potatoes
1 cup light Karo syrup
1 cup white sugar
1 cup water
2 teaspoons vinegar
2 teaspoons cornstarch
1 teaspoon vanilla

Boil potatoes in their "jackets" and cool.
Peel and quarter and place in a 9x13 baking dish.

Combine rest of ingredients in a heavy saucepan.
Bring to a boil.
Turn heat down so mixture continues at a slow boil.
Cook until the mixture changes color (turns light brown) and becomes a little thick.
Sprinkle sweet potatoes with salt and dot with butter.
Pour hot syrup over potatoes.
Bake uncovered for about ½ hour at 350 degrees.
Although the sweet potatoes are great when first served, the syrup gets thicker and soaks into the potatoes more each time they are warmed over!

History of Recipe:
During World War II, Mills Cafeteria in downtown Cincinnati, Ohio served sweet potatoes similar to this recipe. Mills Cafeteria wouldn't give Mrs. Perkins the recipe but she created this recipe to match the taste of the ones served at the cafeteria. She always made these sweet potatoes for Thanksgiving and Christmas dinners. Many a car trunk ended up sticky from the syrup that leaked out of the containers when transporting this dish to various family dinners!

Note: The late Mina Perkins was the author's Mother-in-Law.

Sweet Potato Soufflé
Amy Gwin Thompson

2-1/2 lbs. sweet potatoes
2 beaten eggs
1-2 tablespoons oil
4 tablespoons butter
½ teaspoon ground ginger
1-2 teaspoons allspice
Cinnamon to taste
½ cup coconut sugar
¼ cup full-fat coconut milk
Couple of generous pinches sea salt, divided

Pecan Pie Streusel

1 cup pecans, roughly chopped, coated in 1 teaspoon oil and prebaked on parchment paper 10 minutes in oven
½ cup coconut or brown sugar
½ cup graham crackers
½ cup rolled oats
4 tablespoons real maple syrup
4 tablespoons butter
½ teaspoon cinnamon
Pinch of salt

Preheat oven to 400 degrees.
Slice potatoes in half lengthwise and toss with oil to coat, plus a hefty pinch of sea salt.
Arrange cut-side-down, on a rimmed baking sheet lined with parchment paper.
Bake 35 minutes or until an inserted fork meets no resistance. (Potatoes can be microwaved wrapped in wax paper as well)
Set aside to cool slightly.

Lower oven temperature to 350 degrees.

Sweet Potato Soufflé (cont'd)

While potatoes are baking, heat 6 tablespoons butter in a small saucepan over medium flame.
Add cinnamon, ginger and allspice.
Cook until frothy and light brown, about 5 minutes.
Set aside while you make streusel topping.

Grind oats into a coarse flour in food processor.
Empty into a medium bowl and combine with remaining streusel ingredients.

When baked potatoes are cool enough to handle, remove skins and add potatoes to a large bowl.
Mash potatoes until mostly smooth, then add butter, sugar, coconut milk, 2 beaten eggs and salt.
Mix thoroughly.
Additional seasonings can be added such as thyme, if desired.

Spoon mixture into lightly greased soufflé dish and evenly distribute streusel over the top.
Transfer to a rimmed baking sheet to catch any bubble-ups.
Bake in a 350-degree oven until topping is deeply browned, 35-40 minutes.

Allow to cool slightly before serving.

Enjoy!

Fried Green Tomatoes

Greg & Kim Evans
Crossroads Family Restaurant & Gift Shop
615 West Highway 50
Versailles, IN   47042

Take a large green tomato.

Slice into ¼ inch slices.

Mix flour and Lawry's Seasoned Salt – to taste.

Toss in seasoned flour.

Place in buttermilk and then toss again in seasoned flour.

Place in 350-degree oil for 2 minutes or until golden brown.

Index

Alice Cookies	158
Alice's Chili	388
Alice's Cube Steak and Gravy	216
Alice's Deviled Eggs	344
Angel Waffles	55
Ann Jones' Meat Loaf	224
Apple Butter	188
Apple Cake	60
Apple Dumplings	258
Apple Harvest Bread Pudding	332
Apple Sauce Cake	62
Apricot or Prune Whip	274
Aunt Alice's Potatoes	420
Aunt Isabel's Ginger Bread	32
Aunt Nora's Donuts	34
Aunt Ruby's Biscuits	26
Aunt Ruby's Yeast Rolls	44
Baked Chicken	200
Baked Ham	219
Baked Noodles	259
Baking a Turkey	251
Baklava	275
Banana Bread	24
Banana Cream Pie	292
Banana Split Lasagna	277
Beef Brisket	193
Beef Cheese Ball	13
Beef Marinade	194
Beef Stew	195

Beef Stroganoff	197
Beer Cheese Dip for Round Rye Bread	15
Better Homes & Gardens Corn Bread	30
BIG Nut Rolls	171
Billy's Cowboy Beans	411
Blackberry Cake	63
Blackberry Cake with Coffee	65
Blueberry Angel Dessert	279
Blueberry Angel Food Cake	280
Blueberry Buckle	130
Brato Cake or Hawaiian Cake	67
Braunschweiger Ball	16
Bread	27
Bread Dressing/Stuffing	131
Breakfast Casserole	133
Broccoli Casserole	134
Broccoli-Cauliflower Salad	345
Brownie Supreme	68
Buckeyes	118
Butterfinger Pie	294
Buttermilk Pie	296
Butterscotch Pie	295
Buttery Peanut Brittle	127
Cabbage Au Gratin	135
Cabbage, Sausage & Potato Casserole	136
Candied Sweet Potatoes	428
Caramel Frosted Apple Cake	74
Carrot Cake	69
Cauliflower Soup	386
Charleston Coconut Pie	297
Cheese Straws – Puff Pastry Strips	374
Cheese Stuffed Mushrooms	17
Cherry Cheesecake Lush	154

Cherry Cream Pie	299
Cherry Delight	301
Cherry Delight Pie	300
Cherry Dumplings	260
Cherry Pie	298
Chess Pie	302
Chester Soup	387
Chewy Oatmeal Cookie	175
Chicken and Rice	198
Chicken Casserole Supreme	138
Chicken Inn Fried Chicken	213
Chicken Parisienne	199
Chicken Salad	209
Chili	389
Chili Con Carne	390
Chinese Chews	159
Chocolate Chip Cookies	160
Chocolate Cream Pie	303
Chocolate Éclair Cake	70
Chocolate Skillet Cake with Peanut Butter and Chocolate Icing	72
Chocolate Sundae Cake	76
Chopped Beef Boule'	12
Christmas Tea	182
Cinnamon Pudding	337
Cloud Bread	28
Coconut Macaroons	161
Coconut Pie	305
Corn Bread	29
Corn Bread Pie	139
Corn Chowder	394
Corn Pudding	141
Cornish Hens	215

Cottage Cheese Pie	306
Cranberry Almond Muffins	42
Cranberry Salad	350
Cream Cheese Ball	18
Cream Puffs	283
Cream Roasted Chicken	206
Creamy Mushroom Soup	401
Creamy Vanilla Pudding	341
Crisp Cucumbers	352
Crockpot Cheesy Broccoli Potato Soup	396
Crunchy Fried Chicken	202
Crustless Pumpkin Pie	323
Cry Baby Cookies	163
Custard Bread Pudding	333
Custard Pie	307
Dee Dee's Wedding Salad	353
Delicious Yeast Rolls	56
Dirt Dessert	338
Dot's Pork Chops	237
Dump Cake	78
Easy Chicken Casserole	137
Easy Coconut Macaroons	162
Easy Fantasy Fudge, Option #1	121
Easy Fantasy Fudge, Option #2	122
Easy Peach Cobbler	286
Easy Pot Roast	239
Elephant Ears	36
Enchiladas	217
Favorite Spaghetti Sauce	243
Fish Chowder	395
Five Cup Salad	354
Float Dessert	339
Florida Pie	308

Fluffy Lemon Pie	311
Freezing Bacon	192
French Bread for Bread Machine	31
French Cream	103
Fresh Orange Pound Cake	79
Fresh Strawberry Pie	327
Fried Cheerios	375
Fried Corn	416
Fried Green Tomatoes	431
Friendship Cake	80
Frozen Fruit Salad	355
Fruit Cake	83
Fruit Cocktail Salad Cake	82
Fruited Pot Roast	240
Funnel Cakes	39
Gary's Cheese Ball	14
German Chocolate Pie	309
Gerri's Chicken Pot Pie	208
Gerri's Wildcat Blueberry Cream Puff	281
Gingerbread Cake	86
Glazed Cinnamon Scones	288
Good Pie Crust	318
Good Waffles	57
Gourmet Potatoes	422
Grandma Phyllis' Macaroni Salad	360
Grandma Tolliver's Dill Pickles	417
Grandma's Stack Cake / Cookies	107
Green Bean Bake	143
Green Cookbook Peanut Butter Fudge	124
Green Whipped Salad	356
Grilled Peanut Butter	372
Ham Loaf with Fruit Sauce	220
Hamburger Soup	397

Hans' Pizza	235
Hans' Pork Loin, Pork Shoulder or Brisket	230
Harry's Oatmeal Cookies	173
Hash Brown Breakfast Casserole	144
Herb Baked Turkey	253
Hidden Valley Ranch Oyster Crackers	377
Homemade Chicken or Beef Noodles	261
Homemade Noodles	262
Homemade Pizza	236
Homemade Vanilla Float	342
Homemade Yeast Rolls	45
Honey Bun Cake	87
Honey Mounds	166
Hot Spinach Salad	367
Hush Puppies	40
Hush Puppies	41
Impossible Pie	310
Isabelle's Banana Bread	25
Italian Style Meat Ball Spaghetti	246
Italian Vegetable Soup	406
Jane's Cookies	164
Jell-O Salad	357
JUCA (Traditional Slovak Christmas Soup)	398
Karen Pence's Famous "Next Best Thing to Tom Selleck" Dessert	272
Last Minute Cranberry Relish	349
Lemon Chicken Barbeque	203
Lemon Rice Soup	400
Lemonade Muffins	91
Lemon-Coconut Pound Cake	89
Libby's Famous Pumpkin Pie	322
Light Bread	33
Linda's Easy Blackberry Cobbler	293

Lou Sena Tolliver's Ginger Cookies	165
Louisiana Carrot Salad	359
Love Light Chocolate Cake	90
Mamaw's Rolls	47
Marbaugh Chocolate Cake	71
Mary's Fried Corn	414
Meat Loaf Supreme	225
Mediterranean Chicken	205
Mel's Wine	183
Memphis Mustard Cole Slaw	347
Mexican Fruit Cake	92
Mexican Goulash	218
Mexican Lasagna	223
Mexican Wedding Cookies	167
Microwave Corn on the Cob	413
Million Dollar Pie	315
Miracle Cheese Cake	156
Mocha Berry Tortilla Cups	284
Mom's Cooked Potato Salad Dressing	425
Mom's Easter Tea Ring	53
Mom's Lemon Pie	312
Mom's Noodles and Dumplings	265
Mom's Southern Spoon Bread	50
Monk's Chili	391
Mother's Swedish Chocolate Pudding	336
Muffin Pan Meat Loaves	226
Mushroom Salsa Chili	392
Never Fail Pie Meringue	314
Noodles	263
Noodles and Tomatoes	264
Nut Horns	168
Nut Rolls	169
Nutter Butter Dessert	285

O'Brien Potato Casserole	145
Oatmeal Cake	95
Oatmeal Cake – Betty Lou Ritchie	93
Oatmeal Crisps	174
Oatmeal Pie	316
Old Fashioned Cream Pie	313
Old Fashioned Perfection Salad	365
Old Settler's Baked Beans	410
Opal Tolliver's Cinnamon Bread (Cake)	77
Opal's Zucchini Bread	58
Orange Spiced Sweet Potatoes	427
Oriental Soup	402
Overnight Salad	363
Party Chicken	207
Pasta Salad	362
Pastichio	228
Patricia's Dressing	142
Patricia's Spaghetti	244
Pea Salad	364
Peanut Butter Fudge	123
Peanut Butter Pie	317
Peanut Butter Pudding	340
Pecan Pie Cake	96
Persimmon Cake	97
Pie Pastry	319
Pig Eating Cake	99
Pig Lickin' Cake	98
Pizzelles – an Italian Waffle Cookie	177
Popcorn Balls	378
Popovers	43
Pork and Orange Juice Roast	231
Pork Chops in Sour Cream	238
Pot Pie	419

Potato Salad	423
Potato Salad	424
Potato Salad	426
Potato Soup	403
Potato Soup (Bloodmobile!)	404
Potomac Grilled Oysters	233
Praline French Toast	38
Praline Pecan Crunch	379
Pressure Cooker Beef Stew	196
Pretzel Salad	366
Prize-Winning Chili	393
Pulled Cream Candy	120
Pumpkin Crunch Cake	100
Pumpkin Fudge	125
Pumpkin Pie	321
Puppy Chow	380
Quick Doughnuts	35
Quick Sweet Rolls	52
Raisin Molasses Bars	287
Ralph's Cocktail Sauce	19
Ralph's Wilted Lettuce	358
Red Cake	101
Rice Casserole	146
Rich Italian Spaghetti Sauce	249
Ristoff's Barbecue Ribs	241
Rockin' Broccoli Salad	346
Ruby's Bread Pudding	335
Rum Cake	104
Salmon Patties	242
Sausage Chowder	405
Sausage Muffins	49
Shoo Fly Pie	324
Sloppy Fried Potatoes	421

Snickers Bar Pie	325
Snow Ball Cake	106
Southern Spoon Bread	51
Southwestern Black Bean Salsa	381
Spaghetti Sauce with Meat	245
Spiced Pecans	382
Spicy Tuna Roll	250
Sponge Cake	105
Steven's Haystacks	376
Strawberry Pie	326
Strawberry Smoothie	185
Stuffed Celery	383
Stuffed Green Peppers	418
Sugar Cream Pie - #1	328
Sugar Cream Pie - #2	329
Sugar Molasses Cookies	178
Super Cole Slaw	348
Susan's Shrimp Casserole	147
Sweet Amish Macaroni Salad	361
Sweet Pickled Beets	412
Sweet Potato Casserole #1	148
Sweet Potato Casserole #2	149
Sweet Potato Soufflé	429
Tender Juicy Hamburgers	222
Texas Cake	109
Texas Sheet Cake	110
Thanksgiving Cranberry Mold	351
The Pink Noodle Story	267
Thousand Island Dressing	368
Three Layer Jell-O Salad	369
Thumbprint Cookies	179
Tiropetas	20
Toad in the Hole	150

Tolliver Apple Butter	189
Trail Mix	384
Triple Chocolate Cheesecake	155
Triple-Cheese Macaroni	151
Turkey Pot Pie	254
Vanilla Blueberry Loaf Cake	112
Vanishing Oatmeal Raisin Cookies	176
Vegetable Medley Casserole	152
Vegetable Soup	407
Wanda Huff Fruitcake	85
Warm Ruben Spread	21
White Milk Punch	184
White Walnut Cake	114
Wing Sauce	255
Zucchini Appetizer	22
Zucchini Cake	115

Author Helen Salyer Perkins grew up in a very large extended family where most of the women were excellent cooks, Helen was exposed to many excellent dishes and recipes. As a result, when she married and became mother to three growing and always hungry boys, Helen learned to make delicious – at least most of the time – meals for them. Over the years, she added many and varied recipes and recipe books to her collection.

For two years in the early 2000's, Helen was host of *Kitchen Korner*, a cooking program on WNVI, a local radio station in North Vernon, Indiana. She would review and pass on various recipes to her listeners five days a week. Many days, a guest was in the studio who shared their favorite recipe. A couple of the most memorable guests were former Indiana Governor Edgar Whitcomb and now Vice President of the United States Mike Pence. Both were just delightful and very interesting guests.

Helen was born and grew up in Ohio but moved to Indiana nearly 40 years ago. The boys are grown now and have families of their own, but they contact her frequently to get the recipes for their favorite dishes. The most requested being "Bread Dressing / Stuffing". She has spent the past year sorting and organizing her stash of recipes in a concerted effort to pass them on for others to enjoy!

Milton Keynes UK
Ingram Content Group UK Ltd.
UKHW020724161023
430691UK00005B/29